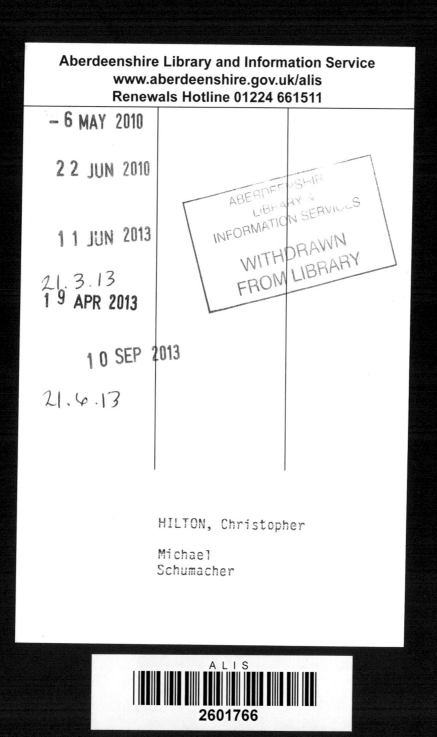

MICHAEL SCHUMACHER

Other titles by Christopher Hilton

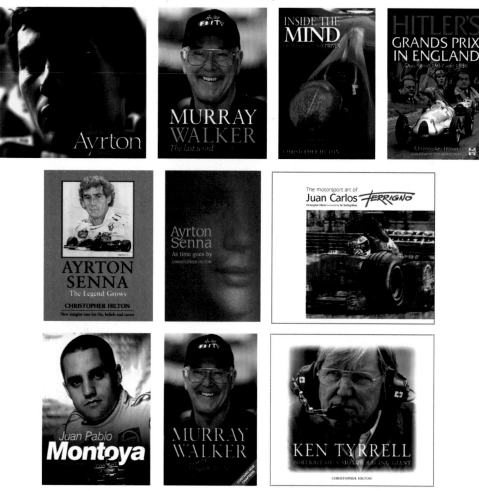

'In order to get the ultimate in performance,
man has always – always – surpassed whatever technology has been provided.'
– Sir Jackie Stewart, discussing Michael Schumacher

MICHAEL SCHUMACHER
THE GREATEST OF ALL

CHRISTOPHER HILTON
Photography by Rainer Schlegelmilch
SECOND EDITION

FULL ANALYSIS OF HIS RECORD-BREAKING SIX WORLD CHAMPIONSHIPS

First published in April 2002
Reprinted September 2002
Second edition November 2003

A catalogue record for this book is available from the
British Library

ISBN 1 84425 044 X

Library of Congress catalog card no. 2003 110431

Haynes North America Inc., 861 Lawrence Drive,
Newbury Park, California 91320, USA.

Published by Haynes Publishing, Sparkford,
Yeovil, Somerset BA22 7JJ, UK.
Tel: 01963 442030 Fax 01963 440001
Int. tel: +44 1963 442030 Int. fax: +44 1963 440001
E-mail: sales@haynes.co.uk
Website: www.haynes.co.uk

Designed by Simon Larkin, Haynes Publishing
Printed and bound in Britain by
J. H. Haynes & Co. Ltd, Sparkford

CONTENTS

History was never far away, whatever Michael Schumacher felt about such notions.

This is Indianapolis and a Maserati 8CTF from the 1930s. Schumacher drove a lap in it.

INTRODUCTION and ACKNOWLEDGEMENTS

The first edition of this book, published at the start of the 2002 season, had a question mark at the end of the title: *Michael Schumacher – The Greatest Of All?* We have the answer now. It is not just the fact that he has won six World Championships, not just the number of wins, pole positions and fastest laps, although these totals are monumental. It is not just the ability to master almost every situation and aspect of technology, not just the renaissance at Ferrari, to which he contributed so much. The greatness is a compound of all this. Schumacher, with Ferrari, established a domination so complete that it threatened the competitive well-being of Formula 1 *and the rules had to be changed.* No other driver has provoked this.

This second edition covers the 2002 and 2003 seasons in detail because Schumacher was pushing into largely unexplored territory. Only two significant records remained to be beaten at the end of 2002 – the five championships of Juan-Manuel Fangio and the 65 pole positions of Ayrton Senna. Both had seemed unassailable, even in an historical context: they might have lasted for generations because only a special conjunction of circumstances could threaten either. Schumacher and Ferrari was that conjunction. In October 2003, he moved past Fangio and Senna's total had come squarely into view. Schumacher would finish 2003 on 55 poles and have a contract with Ferrari through to 2006.

There is an historical feel to the book because it's about Schumacher's place in the life of the World Championship, which began in 1950. He has lifted himself to a level where it is impossible to discuss him in any other terms.

I am particularly thankful to Sir Stirling Moss, Sir Jackie Stewart and Jo Ramirez for giving me long interviews. Jody Scheckter kindly answered three important questions. Jim Endruweit, former Lotus mechanic, provided invaluable background on Jim Clark. Pat Symonds of Benetton made space in his busy schedule to talk at length about Schumacher's first victory.

Paolo Martinelli, the Ferrari engine chief, made the daunting subject of engineering, and Schumacher's relationship with it, simplicity itself. Luca Colajanni, in charge of the team's motorsport press office, provided invaluable background information. Nigel Stepney, a former Lotus mechanic and long-time member of the Ferrari team, was as candid as he always is. Rory Byrne gave a precise précis of the 2001 season.

Many others helped with information, particularly Nigel Roebuck (who allowed me to reproduce a fascinating interview he did with Martin Brundle), Doug Nye, Renaud de Laborderie and Jean-Louis Schlesser. Manuela Borelli of the Ferrari Media Service hunted out material I needed. Biranit Goren kindly allowed me to use two extracts from an interview which *The Atlas F1* website did with Jean Todt.

Stéphane Samson, a French journalist (now with *F1 Racing* magazine), described in detail how Schumacher came to understand the emotion of Ferrari and allowed me to quote from the feature article he wrote about that. The article centred on the 1983 Ferrari which Patrick Tambay had driven and Schumacher would now test. Tambay provided a series of intriguing insights about that day.

Derek Warwick was his usual candid self in describing how – enraged and on foot – he chased, and caught, Schumacher at the Nürburgring in the sportscar days. Gary Anderson of Jordan made Schumacher's first test and first Grand Prix live again, and Ian Phillips, the team's Commercial Manager, filled in important details. Brian Hart helped, as ever, explaining backgrounds and finding contexts.

I'm deeply grateful to David Hayhoe for reading the manuscript and his *Grand Prix Data Book* (with David Holland/Duke, 1997) was an invaluable source of reference. I've also leaned on *Autosport, Autocourse* (Hazleton Publishing) and the *Marlboro Grand Prix Guide.* Claire Williams of Octagon Motorsports dug out a map of Silverstone showing the South Circuit, which was where Schumacher first drove a Formula 1 car, finding himself in a fast and frightening place, not some sculptured mini-track suitable for go-karts. I thank her too.

Chapter One

THE SIXTH KINGDOM

'I am empty and exhausted and just proud of what we all have achieved.'

Michael Schumacher sat alone, perfectly composed, facing a television camera. Looking at him – the face impassive, controlled, almost severe – you'd never know that, a few minutes before, he'd won his sixth World Championship and now inhabited territory where no man had ever been. It seemed to leave him bemused. 'The feelings haven't sunk in. I can well feel for the team but I can't feel for myself at the moment.'

Suzuka on a slate-grey late afternoon, 12 October 2003.

He had finished the Japanese Grand Prix in eighth place, precisely enough to secure him the championship whatever his only rival, Kimi Räikkönen (McLaren), did.

Räikkönen would have had to win the race *and* Schumacher to be lower than eighth for the crown to have been taken by the young Finn. Schumacher's Ferrari team-mate Rubens Barrichello, commanded the race and won it nicely enough so Räikkönen was held in a vice: Barrichello hurting him from the front, Schumacher hurting him from the back.

That is a sanitised summary of Schumacher's 1 hour 26 minutes and 11.230 seconds at Suzuka. He said it had been one of his hardest races and, he might have added, a shifting mosaic of chance, luck and hard racing, with nothing certain.

But now, facing the camera, he did what he had always done since joining Ferrari in 1996 and that was to be a team player. He said that he wanted to mention his colleagues, not himself and 'repeat it ever so often. Today they have done an incredible job giving both of us a car where we have been at all times competitive.'

Outside, his wife Corinne almost bubbled over. She wore a hat with 'Six Times World Champion' on it but said Michael didn't know anything about that. He'd have been annoyed at any tempting of providence, and he had his reasons.[1] She thought it would take him a few days to really grasp what he had achieved.

A great irony in that. Like many modern drivers, Schumacher professed a minimal interest in yesterday, or indeed records. Likely as not he knew nothing about 4 August 1957 when Juan-Manuel Fangio (Maserati) won the German Grand Prix by 3.6 seconds from Mike Hawthorn (Ferrari) and simultaneously won his fifth World Championship. It took Fangio 3 hours 30 minutes 38.300 seconds, but that was the way it was then.

The five titles stood as the ultimate motor racing record, and it might have lasted a hundred years. That was the true measure of Fangio's greatness. In all the time between the Nürburgring and Suzuka only one man, Alain Prost, had approached it, with four. To equal it seemed highly unlikely – Grand Prix racing is too unpredictable, periods of domination by one driver and one team are usually too short. To beat it was fantasy. The five was the record that was always going to be out of reach, a sort of immense monument standing alone, unassailable.

And then the son of a working man from an anonymous German town came.

Schumacher and Fangio had met. In 1991, at the Norisring, a 1.4m (2.3km) circuit on the outskirts of Nuremberg, they 'drove' together in what was called a retrospective: a day for people to watch old and venerated cars. Schumacher was lean and short-haired, with the smile of a young man. Not surprising. He was 22 and had reached the World Sportscar Championship with Mercedes.

Wolfgang Schattling – former English teacher, journalist and then Mercedes Press Officer – was at the Norising. 'Yes,

The 2003 season had a difficult start. Pit stop power in Australia, as the quest for the sixth title begins – but Schumacher was only fourth.

Smokescreen in Brazil – and later he'd crash.

he had heard of Fangio and he was impressed by him. There was an aura about Fangio which you couldn't miss, and Schumacher didn't miss it.'

They drove two or three laps side-by-side. Schumacher had the W154, from 1939, and Fangio the W196 with which he had won the 1955 World Championship. It was controlled, as these things are – a celebration not a competition, safe, rather stately and no bad place for a 22-year-old to be.

Later in this book I shall be comparing Schumacher's achievements in Formula 1 with Fangio's. Here I simply want to make the point that there *is* a continuity within Formula 1, as with everything else, no matter how much the eras differ. Fangio was born in 1911 and last drove in a Grand Prix in 1958, eleven years before Schumacher was born. Yet there they are at the Norisring having their photograph taken, Fangio almost grave, Schumacher with that almost boyish smile, hands on hips.

However much Schumacher professes that the past holds no particular appeal or relevance, he cannot escape the continuity because he is a product of it. The World Championship did not begin with him, it began in 1950 and was itself an evolution from the mighty 1930s which were themselves an evolution from the end of the previous century when 'horseless carriages' raced each other on public roads.

It is the continuity which demands that we seek Schumacher's place within motorsport history – something absolutely necessary after the sixth championship – and that leads to an immediate paradox.

From his Grand Prix debut at Ferrari (Australia, 1996) to his fifth World Championship (France, 2002) driver and team built continually, so that each climactic was but a step towards the next, and this culminated in a strength so great that it became the weakness. Nothing like it had been seen before. Between 2000 and 2002 Schumacher won 29 races. Fangio, in his whole career, won 24. It's not that simple, of course, and we'll be exploring the complexities in due course – but you cannot ignore the 29 victories any more than the continuity.

The Schumacher-Ferrari completeness had taken him to

equalling Fangio's five titles in 2002 but, as mentioned in the Introduction, if prolonged this would threaten the whole edifice because the multi-national companies in Formula 1 all wanted to parade their wares before a global television audience. What happened when the audience stopped watching because Schumacher won all the time and the races were barely competitive?

For 2003, extensive rule changes were introduced to shake the whole thing up and that made Schumacher's attempt on Fangio's monument *much* more interesting. In brief: qualifying became a one-run shoot-out, and the cars had on board the fuel they'd start the race with. The points were extended and bunched (10-8-6-5-4-3-2-1), the 2 points from first to second making it more difficult for Schumacher to romp into the distance. Team orders were banned and electronic aids due to be phased out. Ferrari's tactical supremo, Ross Brawn[2] would say, discussing the rule changes, that 'nothing ... favoured Ferrari one jot. There wasn't one decision in our interests. We were dominating Formula 1, we had everything together, a good way of working and it all got turned upside down.'

Even so, when the new Ferrari (the F2003-GA) was launched it seemed to be the next step forward. Although it hadn't turned a wheel, designer Rory Byrne said: 'Last year I predicted that the F2002 would prove to be the best Ferrari F1 car ever and it proved to be the most successful. We have not yet run the F2003 but so far all our performance objectives have been reached or exceeded, so I am confident the F2003-GA will be the best Ferrari F1 car ever.'

Confidence was the theme of the launch and, just for a moment, you thought that even the new rules might not be enough. Schumacher drove the car for the first time at Fiorano on 11 February, covered 78 laps and pronounced himself happy. It was due to make its Grand Prix debut at Imola, fourth race of the season.

By then, of course, Schumacher might be well on his way towards the uninhabited territory, the place where no man had been.

Australia, the first race, went wrong although he took pole. As it seems, Ferrari didn't make the right tyre choice – the weather was distinctly mixed – and he hit a kerb hard enough to damage the car. He finished fourth. The question reared: to bring the new car to Malaysia. Brawn rejected that, saying that what happened during the Melbourne race would have happened regardless of which car they had.

Schumacher qualified third in Malaysia and finished the race sixth, a lap down. 'It was a tough race with an unfortunate start. I made a mistake and hit Jarno [Trulli] and I have apologised to him. That was the decisive moment.' This happened on the second corner and 'it came as a big surprise that I was still able to drive for points after the drive-through penalty, so I am happy enough in the circumstances.'

He qualified seventh in Brazil, a wet race, but aquaplaned into a crash. Significantly, he said 'the gap to the championship leader is not so big, given there are still 13 races, so there is no need to be concerned about it.' For perspective, he pointed out that 'this is my first non-finish since Hockenheim in 2001.' That, of course, was due to the reliability of the car as much as to Schumacher's ability to keep it out of trouble but, in a very real sense, it *was* the completeness.

The championship was led by Räikkönen (26 points) from team-mate David Coulthard (15) and Fernando Alonso (Renault, 14). Schumacher had 8.

The F2003 did not go to Imola...

Instead – with his mother critically ill in Germany – he flew to her bedside after taking pole for the San Marino Grand Prix. Brother Ralf[3] went with him.

Their mother died.

They raced, and Schumacher won. Team boss Jean Todt said: 'This was a special victory. Michael proved yet again, even to those who do not seem to accept it, that he is a special man. Despite being in mourning, he wanted to take part in this race for the sake of the team and went on to win it. Then, going onto the podium, he wanted to acknowledge all the team and our fans who love him as much as we do. We have gone through some very stressful moments and Michael appreciated the way the team supported him. It is at

Opposite: Imola and the win that opened up the championship after three difficult races.

The reign in Spain fell mainly as champagne on Barrichello and young Fernando Alonso, too.

moments like these that the values we hold dear and cultivate in the team come to the fore.'

He did take the F2003 to Spain, took pole – and the race; took pole in Austria and won it despite a cockpit fire at a pit stop. 'I could see the fire. Maybe the mechanics thought I was cold and wanted to warm me up! But the team did a good job to control the situation, reacting quickly with the extinguishers.'

Räikkönen still led the championship with 40 points, Schumacher next on 38, Barrichello 26. Grand Prix racing was alive again, and more so after Monaco where he qualified fifth and finished third. Montoya won, the fifth winner in seven races.

On 9 June, between Monaco and Canada, Ferrari announced that the senior executives in their team – Todt, Brawn, Paolo Martinelli, Rory Byrne, head of engine design Gilles Simon – and Schumacher would all be staying until the end of the 2006 season. The assumption was that

No magic at Monaco, where Schumacher was third.

Schumacher would drive until then (rather than take a role such as ambassador for the company or technical adviser) and that put every leading Grand Prix record at his mercy. He would set totals never seen before and maybe never to be seen again because of a conjunction of factors: Schumacher's range of skills and Ferrari's ability to hire the people they wanted, then forge it all into a team. To this must be added stability: the team was given time and massive funding.

At every public opportunity you'd hear Ferrari F1 people – but most notably Schumacher – extolling the virtues of the team and, in his early days there, it sounded exactly like the sort of incantation all well-trained drivers repeat. You hear it so often that it becomes a *given*: they all pay homage to their teams (and their engine manufacturers and their tyre manufacturers), constantly.

At Ferrari, this was quite different. They were not just going Grand Prix racing: they were in the process of creating something momentous. This had already risen to a level unequalled in motor racing history *and they were all working to keep it improving.* That's why they spoke sincerely about the team. That's why Ross Brawn talks

quite naturally about Schumacher the team-builder and team-player.

You have seen this in the *parc fermé* when Schumacher's just won a race and members of the team are crowded on the other side of the fence. He observes certain niceties, as decorum demands, congratulating whichever drivers have finished second and third and then goes to the team and salutes as many as he can physically with embraces, hugs, high-fives – all *tactile* gestures. He is saying *we* won that race. Whenever you see it, you are not seeing a stage performance but something strong and real.

He qualified third in Canada and won the race despite concerns about his brakes. 'I had to be careful to look after them so I did not push too hard at first. I only really pushed hard in the period around the pit stops.' Todt murmured that it had been an 'incredible race,' and that judgement inadvertently covered a broader terrain than he intended.

There's a hallowed phrase in Grand Prix racing: the great ones can *drive round a problem,* meaning that if something happens to their car they have enough spare mental and physical capacity to be able to adjust so that, although the problem remains, they continue competitive. Jim Clark could do this. Ayrton Senna also. As a young man he won a Formula 3 race having lost his front brakes completely. Michael Schumacher covered a goodly part of the 1994 Spanish Grand Prix with his Benetton stuck in fifth gear and still finished second (see Chapter Four). The problem was not so dramatic in Canada, so he drove round it and won.

Now the season began to tighten again. He qualified second at the European Grand Prix at the Nürburgring (Räikkönen pole) and finished fifth after a 'moment' when Juan Pablo Montoya (Williams) took him at the hairpin on lap 43. He described the 'collision' as a straightforward racing incident. 'He was faster than me, tried to pass, and gave me just enough room to survive. Maybe I could have wished for a little bit more space but I have no problems with Juan Pablo over this.' Ralf won, and the points had become Schumacher 58, Räikkönen 51, Ralf 43, Montoya and Alonso 39.

The new rules, combined with the improvement of McLaren and Williams, had changed everything. Only the season before, Schumacher had gone to France leading his team-mate Barrichello 86–32 and taken the championship. True, the race had been the eleventh of 2002 and was only the tenth of 2003 but that does not diminish the central point.

Ralf took France (Schumacher third) and Barrichello took Silverstone (Schumacher fourth) so that with five races left Schumacher had 69 points, Räikkönen 62, Montoya 55, Ralf 53, Barrichello 49. Schumacher was running second in Germany when a left rear tyre punctured near the end. Montoya won and was now in prime form.

Schumacher qualified eighth in Hungary and was beset by all manner of problems while Alonso won by commanding the race from the front. His time: 1h 39m 01.46s. Schumacher finished eighth, a lap down. He'd spent 'a lot of time stuck behind a slower car'. Hungary was being viewed within Ferrari as a debacle because, too, Barrichello's left rear wheel had suddenly come off.

The championship had become Schumacher 72, Montoya 71, Räikkönen 70, Ralf 58. Schumacher said 'I love fighting' and that he still 'believed in our possibilities'. That could not disguise the fact that a sense of uncertainty – perhaps even of self-doubt – was permeating Ferrari while such as Montoya and Räikkönen circled for the kill.

There were three weeks to the Italian Grand Prix and a major test session at Monza before that. Schumacher tested from 2 September (30 laps, setting the best time of the day at 1m 22.524s). Ralf crashed so heavily in the Williams that he was taken to hospital and, as it proved, that destroyed any lingering chance of the title that he had.

Meanwhile the test session heated up. On 3 September Schumacher did 60 laps (best 1m 22.131s), next day 79 laps (1m 21.286s), the day after that 61 laps. Here are the final times (Marc Gene deputising for Ralf):

Schumacher	1m 20.730s
Barrichello	1m 20.850s
Montoya	1m 21.054s
Gene	1m 21.488s
Coulthard	1m 21.546s
Räikkönen	1m 21.710s

Drawing big conclusions from any test session is problematic but Schumacher did take, as he was entitled to do, confidence from the week at Monza. He pointed out that up until the British Grand Prix – only three races back – the Ferrari had been the 'car to beat' so its intrinsic qualities were not in doubt. However 'we' – by implication the team as well as himself – didn't 'get everything' out of the car in Germany or Hungary. He fully intended to do that in the Monza race, which, all else aside, might well be the fastest Grand Prix ever run.

Montoya was quickest on the Friday, from Barrichello and Schumacher. Qualifying on the Saturday distilled the season.

Räikkönen went fifth last and constructed a neat, self-contained lap which belied its speed. **1m 21.466.**

Cristiano da Matta (Toyota) provided something approaching light relief with 1m 22.914 before Schumacher took it on. He constructed a lap tightly held between precision and throwing the car. His first sector time (25.995s) was decisively ahead of Räikkönen's (26.202) and the Italian crowd adored that. Schumacher carried that

speed through the second sector (27.793/Räikkönen 28.021) and he pumped that up on the run for home. **1m 20.963,** half a second faster than Räikkönen.

Barrichello went next and thought his brakes might not have 'been up to temperature'. **1m 21.242.** Montoya was armed with the mighty BMW engine, and hadn't he set the fastest lap ever driven here last year? He forced the Williams to 25.992 on the first sector, and that was .003 quicker. He forced it to 27.720 on the second sector, and that was .073s quicker, but slight imprecision on his run for home cost him pole. **1m 21.014.** Schumacher had it by 0.051 over 3.6 miles (5.7km).

Now listen to Schumacher: 'We have turned the situation around thanks to the hard work of everyone in the team and at the factory. Our President [di Montezemolo] has helped us to focus on the problems we experienced in the last two races, but we have not been put under any extra pressure here. We have made

Opposite: The beautiful win at Monza, keeping the championship very much alive.

Giving Schumacher as dry a surface as possible for his pit stop at Indianapolis.

improvements to all areas of the car and Bridgestone has given us a very good tyre.'

This is seemingly not publicity-speak but entirely sincere, the *verbal* equivalent of the tactile contact he has with the team. Just as a Formula 1 car depends on every tiny component functioning properly and dies when one does not, the team thrives through the efforts of several hundred people and is, arguably, only as strong as the weakest of them. Perhaps the ultimate Schumacher trick was – by word and touch – to inspire the weakest to be stronger.

The start at Monza is highly pressured because the surge from the grid to the first chicane is so long and wide, and the chicane itself so tight, despite reshaping and refining over the years. It's like pouring a kettle of boiling water into a narrow funnel. You can get scalded.

As the red lights went off Schumacher moved straight ahead and clear, Montoya on his right and pulling in behind as they reached the funnel. Schumacher went in too deep – 'I made a mistake' – and, even at this speed and pressure, weighed two options coldly, short-cutting the chicane or scrambling round. He chose to scramble.

The pit stop fire in Austria, 2003. When it was extinguished, he went back out – and won.

They went round the *Curva Grande* horseshoe like that but into the second chicane – a left-right – Schumacher moved over to protect the racing line. He found Montoya outside him. Montoya squeezed *into* the corner so that Schumacher rode the kerbing and Montoya moved ahead by half a car's length. Montoya clipped a kerb and was pitched over towards Schumacher, squeezing him again, but the clip had given the impetus back to Schumacher. Coming out, Schumacher held mid-track and Montoya searched for a way back at him. Schumacher described this as a 'good fight, hard and fair'.

Montoya would speak of making a good start, seeing the chance to try and pass 'but he had better acceleration than me. We competed cleanly – neither of us could afford not to finish.' These had been muscular, masculine moments, the hungry Colombian measuring himself against the old master, and the old master resisting on and on, to the end. It was as if Schumacher was saying *you might have got*

yourself into the throne room, but you're not having the throne, young man.

It was, Schumacher judged (untypically) 'the greatest day of my career. It was a beautiful and emotional feeling on the podium. The result is also a relief. We believed in ourselves and we knew we could fight back. The championship' – Schumacher 82, Montoya 79, Räikkönen 75 – 'is still very open. We have improved and we keep on improving. The engine guys have done a tremendous job and that should help us in the last two races.'

He and wife Corinne stopped off at Las Vegas on the way to the next race, the USA Grand Prix at Indianapolis. 'We were invited to a show and it fitted in with things well. No one recognised me, except for a few European holidaymakers.' He took on the slot machines but only with small change, and he didn't win.

Indianapolis ought to have favoured Montoya, who won the Indy 500 there in 2000, said the place felt like home and would have vociferous support from a large Colombian contingent in the crowd.

In first qualifying Schumacher was only eighth. He'd had to go first, the running order decided of course by the finishing positions at Monza. He judged this a disadvantage, 'especially after the rain which fell in the morning, which meant the track was a bit dirty and lacked grip'. Next day he qualified seventh and wasn't sure what had gone wrong or why it had gone wrong. Räikkönen had pole, Montoya fourth. This is how Schumacher rationalised it: 'At least seventh place is on the clean side of the track, which is better than being on the dirty inside line. In terms of the championship, my closest rival is only three places ahead of me, so this is not a disaster and with Kimi on pole the race is a bit more open now.'

The race was described by Jean Todt as 'incredibly intense' and that's almost an understatement. Schumacher made a confident start and took fourth, ahead of Montoya. Räikkönen led. It was all deceptively normal – and then Montoya and Barrichello collided. Barrichello went off and couldn't get back on. 'We were running side by side. I thought I had left him enough space but he touched me and

Suzuka 2003.
Top left: *The paddock. All he had to do in Japan was maintain his balance.*

Above: *Now listen, young man: with Takuma Sato – and they'd meet again in the race.*

Top right: *Set piece dialogue before the action began: Schumacher and the only man who could take the title from him, Kimi Räikkönen.*

Above: *Schumacher's plight is evident at Turn One. He's top left in the picture and struggling.*

I spun.' At that moment rain began, bringing uncertainty with it.

On lap 4, Schumacher was still fourth and 3.8 seconds behind Räikkönen. Schumacher cut past Olivier Panis (Toyota) and Montoya charged. The rain was heavier and initially that favoured the cars with Michelin because their dry tyres were better in the wet than Bridgestone, and Schumacher had Bridgestone. Coulthard sailed past Schumacher, swiftly followed by Montoya and Alonso. The rain eased and then stopped – and Montoya was under investigation by the Stewards for the Barrichello collision.

On lap 9, Schumacher was in sixth place and more than eleven seconds behind Räikkönen. It is at these moments that he seems capable of reshaping reality to his will.

He set fastest lap, Montoya's pit stop went wrong – a fuel rig failed – and rain fell again. By now the pit stops were coming in a flurry. Schumacher led briefly then pitted himself. 'We decided to stay with dry tyres but the rain got stronger as I came into the pit lane and I did suggest changing the choice. But it would have been too much of a mess so I came straight back in [next lap].'

Montoya got a drive-through penalty, and at *that* moment his championship was over.

Schumacher was now on Bridgestone intermediates, and they were superior to anything Michelin had. Ralf went off, the conditions forced Räikkönen and Alonso in to change tyres and Schumacher prepared to seize the race. He was seventh, and that became sixth when he moved past Coulthard. He was eleven seconds away from the lead. He moved past Alonso and Justin Wilson (Jaguar) on the same lap. He caught Räikkönen and took him on the inside. Jenson Button (BAR) led from Heinz-Harald Frentzen (Sauber). Schumacher lapped Montoya, moved on Frentzen – but the rain was stopping. Schumacher swept inside Frentzen and was only four seconds from Button. He cut into that, tracked Button down the start-finish straight towards the right-hander, went out onto the *wet* part of the track and went by. This was no longer a motor race: it was a master class.

Schumacher stroked the car home but Button's car broke down so that when Räikkönen overtook Frentzen it was for second place. The championship was still alive, although it had been reduced to a great simplicity. Räikkönen had to win the Japanese Grand Prix and Schumacher get no point. It meant Räikkönen was spared any mental arithmetic. 'Only first place is really worth winning, so I'll drive as hard as I can.'

There's a slightly unreal feel about Suzuka. The circuit is next to a fairground and, behind the grandstand opposite the pits, there's a big bazaar of stalls selling food, drink, memorabilia and, this October, T-shirts saying *Michael Schumacher 6 times World Champion.* Aye, tempting providence although reportedly Schumacher never did see them. The hotel where the drivers stay is set in parkland beyond the bazaar and if he'd ventured there he'd have been mobbed so he drove to the circuit instead.

In first qualifying he was third, Räikkönen fifth. Schumacher had to go first (again) because of the win at Indianapolis and judged that 'a slight disadvantage' so he was 'quite happy with my lap and my time'. Second qualifying proved a roulette wheel, as if motor racing was saying *I can play devilish games with you, just as I have done down all these decades with all the others.*

Montoya did 1:32.412 and Barrichello, out next, did 1:31.713. That was fastest of the session and Alonso couldn't get near it. He did 1:33.044 – fifth. Drizzle fell, and Räikkönen took it on but the change in track conditions slowed him to 1:33.272 – seventh. Schumacher, impassive, watched a monitor from the cockpit deep within the Ferrari garage. Coulthard, next, took that seventh place from Räikkönen while Schumacher circled, preparing for his run. Everybody knew that the Bridgestone tyres did not like a track which was moving from dry to wet.

At the first split, just over half a minute in, Schumacher was 1.008 seconds off Barrichello's provisional pole time, an enormous difference in context; and 2.034 off at the second split, again enormous in context. He crossed the line in 1:34.302 – fourteenth. He hadn't been this far down a grid since Spa in 1995 when he'd been sixteenth (and won from there). Räikkönen was eighth and said, in his hush-whisper voice, that at least Schumacher wasn't in front of him. Schumacher described the conditions as 'inconsistent' and the session as 'interesting'. Dry, nearly wry, understatement was his favoured method of communication, which is why he tried to make a joke about the fire in Austria. He added: 'Everybody knows I love a challenge but [smile] it's an unpredictable challenge. We have to see the whole picture and having one car – Rubens – on the front row is ideal for us.'

As the red lights blinked off, the grid broke up on the long run towards turn one, Barrichello in the lead but Schumacher – over to the right – lost in the pack. As Barrichello turned in, Schumacher was thirteenth. He ran twelfth out of turn one. The race would be run in two distinct dimensions, far apart but constantly affecting each other. In one, Räikkönen had to get up into the lead; in the other, Schumacher had to get up into eighth.

Montoya attacked Barrichello and fled past into the distance. At lap 2, he was 3.4 seconds ahead of Barrichello, Räikkönen sixth at 6.0.

The moment Schumacher answered history on a grey late afternoon, 12 October 2003.

Schumacher was still twelfth but he had Wilson, Takumo Sato (BAR) and Mark Webber (Jaguar) within reach. Immediately he moved inside Wilson and advanced towards Sato. On lap 7, he made a limp, hesitant attempt to squeeze past Sato into the final chicane and was never near to doing it. Sato turned in and Schumacher clipped the BAR's rear. He pitted for a new nosecone and was stationary for 18.1. The championship had been brutally wrenched open. He rejoined nineteenth, only a Minardi behind.

Räikkönen was some fifteen seconds away from Montoya with Barrichello, Alonso and da Matta in between but Montoya's hydraulics failed so that Barrichello inherited the lead and everybody moved up a place. Da Matta pitted, and that made Räikkönen third.

Schumacher, eighteenth, set fastest lap but, without taking into account all the cars in between, he was more than 40 seconds behind Sato in eighth.

At lap 11, Räikkönen was 14.641 seconds behind Barrichello, Alonso still between them. Barrichello and Alonso pitted together and so, fleetingly, Räikkönen led.

Schumacher was sixteenth.

Räikkönen had to pit and that returned the lead to Barrichello – Räikkönen stationary for 9.2, which seemed to indicate only two stops. Barrichello would be making three…

At lap 16 Schumacher was fourteenth, Nick Heidfeld (Sauber) immediately ahead, then Ralf. He hunted Heidfeld down and at the final chicane eased through. Thirteenth.

Räikkönen ran fourth and Alonso stopped out on the circuit with an engine problem so everybody moved up a place. Räikkönen, heavy with fuel, was 20.107 seconds behind Barrichello, with – now – Coulthard in between. Clearly Coulthard would cede the position to his team-mate whenever necessary.

Schumacher was eleventh and Webber pitted. Tenth. Sato and Ralf were wrestling and Schumacher hunted Ralf down, then both of them pitted. They emerged in the same order they'd gone in, Ralf still ahead.

Barrichello pitted, emerged 8.0 in front of Räikkönen.

Schumacher tried to mount an attack on Ralf, but Ralf passed Olivier Panis (Toyota) and Schumacher did too, at the final chicane, just as he'd done Heidfeld.

Barrichello was widening the gap to Räikkönen, who pitted, as did Button.

Amidst all this, Schumacher ran sixth, had to pit again, was stationary for 7.6 and rejoined tenth. Just this once, reality seemed to be reshaping him. Da Matta and Ralf pitted and, as they emerged, Schumacher slotted the Ferrari between them. The crucible of the championship was at hand. Ralf would clearly show brotherly love and, with nothing remaining in the race for him, deference too. He didn't. He attacked so vehemently that down the start-finish straight, Schumacher had to veer across to keep him at bay.

Barrichello pitted a last time, with a 21 seconds lead over Coulthard. That gave Coulthard a temporary lead – when he'd pitted he emerged behind Räikkönen.

On lap 41, at the final chicane, da Matta braked and Schumacher – probing the inside – locked brakes, the wheels churning white smoke. He lurched to the left, into Ralf's path. Under his own braking, Ralf lurched to the left

too and touched the Ferrari's rear wheel. Ralf's front wing broke and Schumacher had to plough a furrow across the grass beyond the chicane to get back on the track. He didn't gain a place doing that, so there was no question of him being penalised but was the Ferrari damaged? He'd flat-spotted his tyres – when you lock wheels you scrub flat the rubber in contact with the track – and, from here on, it felt like driving over kerbing. 'The vibration was so bad I had

vision problems down the straight. I was also worried about a puncture and I was just trying to get the car to the flag.' Brawn would say that 'we were lucky to get away with the incident at the chicane. I guess da Matta must have braked early because Michael almost hit him.'

Schumacher, eighth, attacked da Matta.

Barrichello led Räikkönen by 16.4 seconds.

With five laps to go, the Barrichello–Räikkönen gap was

16.3. Barrichello kept 'pushing' because rain had been forecast and even at three laps from the end, that could spoil everything.

Schumacher let da Matta go and eased off, did get the car to the flag. On the final lap he found himself in the place where nobody had been before. A paradox of historical proportions: Schumacher reached it the instant Barrichello crossed the line to win the race and deprive Räikkönen. The fact that Schumacher was still out at the back of the circuit didn't matter at all.

Now Schumacher approached the line, dipped the car across to the Ferrari mechanics on the pit wall, continued down the straight. Usually, he'd fling the car towards the mechanics and punch the air with both fists as if an explosion was happening within him and, maybe, make the car wriggle violently left-right, left-right. At Suzuka, it all felt strange – his word. Eventually, somewhere past turn one, he raised his right arm from the cockpit and waved it, then shook his head in a sort of wonder.

The strangeness deepened. He was not entitled to a place on the race winners' podium and, instead, had an amicable word with Sato. He had a champagne fight in the Ferrari pit. He sat, faced the camera and described his emotional confusion. He retraced the race, describing how he felt anything could happen at the front and so he had to make sure of it himself. 'You have to think about the worst to be safe.'

Then the party began.

There must have been many good men and true looking down on it.

NOTES

[1] In 1997, Schumacher's manager Willi Weber had a reported 50,000 caps ready for the final race, proclaiming him three times World Champion. Schumacher crashed.

[2] *Autosport*, 25 September 2003.

[3] For simplicity, I have referred to Michael as Schumacher, and his brother as Ralf.

Facts of the matter

One way to understand what Schumacher achieved at Ferrari is to set out what every other driver who drove there achieved too. Somehow memory is distorted by emotion so that the very name Ferrari conjures a vista of great drivers beating the world; somehow memory lacks the objectivity to see how difficult these drivers found it and, in many cases, how little they achieved. Consider that, from 1950, in terms of wins only three drivers got into double figures, and in terms of poles only four. Nor does the list below encompass the 38 men who drove for Ferrari and didn't win once. That is slightly misleading because some of the 38 didn't drive much for Ferrari, but it does emphasise the difficulty.

The list throws into starkest relief what Schumacher has done at Ferrari. He has won an astonishing 51 of his 125 races compared to, in alphabetical order, Michele Alboreto's three wins from 80 races, Jean Alesi's one win from 80 races, and Gerhard Berger's five wins from 96 races. You can argue that the Ferrari infrastructure was not of the quality in the 1980s and early to mid 1990s that it became under Todt and Brawn, and you can argue that the cars were not of the quality to win races.

Let's examine that. In 1995 Ferrari fielded Berger and Alesi. Berger took one pole position and won no races, Alesi took no poles but won Canada. In 1996 Schumacher came and took four poles, three wins. His team-mate Eddie Irvine had no poles and no wins. It was very simple: Schumacher could take a car which was nowhere near good enough to win a World Championship and find ways to make it win races. The others couldn't. So here is the list of drivers who won a Grand Prix for Ferrari.

Note: the years next to each driver indicate that he raced at least once for Ferrari that season. The hyphen, as in 1984–1988, indicates that he drove for the team continuously during that period.

	Years	Races	Poles	Wins	Championship
Alboreto, M	1984-88	80	2	3	0
Alesi, J	1991-95	80	1	1	0
Andretti, M	1971-72/82	12	1	1	0
Arnoux, R	1983-85	32	4	3	0
Ascari, A	1950-54	27	13	13	2
Baghetti, G	1961-62/66	8	0	1	0
Bandini, L	1962/63-67	35	1	1	0
Barrichello, R	2000-03	65	8	7	0
Berger, G	1987-89/93-95	96	7	5	0
Brooks, T	1959	7	2	2	0
Collins, P	1956-58	20	1	3	0
Fangio, J-M	1956	7	5	3	1
Farina, G	1952-55	20	3	1	0
Gonzalez, F	1951/54-55/57/60	15	3	2	0
Hawthorn, M	1953-54/55/57-58	35	4	3	1
Hill, P	1958-60/61-62	31	6	3	1
Ickx, J	1968/70-73	55	11	6	0
Irvine, E	1996-99	65	0	4	0
Lauda, N	1974-77	57	23	15	2
Mansell, N	1989-90	31	3	3	0
Musso, L	1956-58	15	0	1	0
Pironi, D	1981-82	25	2	2	0
Prost, A	1990-91	30	0	5	0
Regazzoni, C	1970-72/74-76	58	4	4	0
Reutemann, C	1976-78	34	2	5	0
Scarfiotti, L	1963-67	6	0	1	0
Scheckter, J	1979-80	28	1	3	1
Schumacher, M	1996-2003	125	45	51	4
Surtees, J	1963-66	30	5	4	1
Tambay, P	1982-83	21	4	2	0
Taruffi, P	1951-55	13	0	1	0
Trintignant, M	1954-55/57	17	0	1	0
Villeneuve, G	1977-82	66	2	6	0
Von Trips, W	1957-58/59-60/61	25	1	2	0

DECISIVE BATTLES (1): SPA, 1991

History is not an exact science, and that's why recreating some aspects of Michael Schumacher's entry into Grand Prix racing remains tantalising and unresolved.[1] It is no less fascinating for that, and the essential element – a lean, angular young man suddenly announcing himself on the global stage – still carries the force that it did at the time. From those August days a decade and more ago, all else flowed: the wins, the championships, Ferrari, the records.

Quite possibly the whole thing began on some unremembered day in Spain, and a conversation between two men who had villas there: Eddie Jordan and Dave Price. Jordan, of course, owned a Formula 1 team. Price had worked for Mercedes, where Schumacher was competing in the World Sports Car Championship. Jordan had antennae in his mind which, even from afar, constantly felt the currents which young drivers emitted and, depending on the strength of the currents, hired some of them. From that they moved on to populate many successful teams.

Jordan asked what this Schumacher was like and Price replied 'bloody good!'

Schumacher had karted from 1984 to 1987, moved through the junior formula Koenig to German Formula 3 in 1989 and then, in 1990, combined that Formula 3 with the Mercedes team in the World Sports Car Championship. There seems little doubt even then that the ultimate object was Formula 1. Early in 1990, as we shall hear in the next chapter, Adrian Reynard – who was trying to set up a

A slender lad, preparing to change Formula 1 forever.

Formula 1 team – had Schumacher down at his factory.

Now, in mid-1991, Schumacher was still with Mercedes and there were already rumours that he'd be joining the Tyrrell team; but Tyrrell had Honda engines and Aguri Suzuki was expected to replace the retiring Satoru Nakajima, for all the obvious reasons. Tyrrell denied the Schumacher connection.[2]

On 28 July Schumacher made his Formula 3000 début at Sugo, Japan, and finished second (to the American Ross Cheever). The drive was arranged by Jochen Neerpasch of Mercedes and Schumacher said at the time: 'Obviously I want to do Formula 1 next year, but whether I can or not is another question. Mr. Neerpasch has a lot of experience and I think he can help me.' The 3000 drive was a one-off and it didn't particularly impress Jordan, whose antennae reached comfortably to Japan. The factor which had 'turned me on,' Jordan would say, was what Schumacher had done in German Formula 3 and the manner of his doing it.

Schumacher at Le Mans where he raced a Mercedes in the 24-hour sports car race just weeks before he made his 1991 Grand Prix début.

A week after that, the Tyrrell rumours surfaced again, because Tyrrell had the German company Braun as a name sponsor and they, evidently, wanted a German driver. The rumour now was that some late autumn day Tyrrell would test Schumacher, Heinz-Harald Frentzen and Bernd Schneider. In the great, unending motor racing stories of what-might-have-been, there is another chapter.

On Sunday 11 August, Ayrton Senna (McLaren) won the Hungarian Grand Prix. Jordan's two drivers, Andrea de Cesaris and Bertrand Gachot, finished seventh and ninth respectively although, reportedly, the Jordan motorhome was heavy with visitors looking for a 1992 drive – Suzuki, Pierluigi Martini, Michael Andretti and, more improbably,

Keke Rosberg, the former World Champion who had retired in 1986.

On the Tuesday, Gachot appeared at Southwark Crown Court, London, accused of spraying CS gas into the face of a taxi driver. The alleged offence had taken place the previous December. On the Wednesday Gachot was jailed for 18 months.

As it happened, a major Formula 1 test was going on at Monza but Jordan, of course, only had de Cesaris there. Gachot had been so sure he'd be acquitted that he intended to fly down to Monza for the test – it lasted until the Friday. More important, the Belgian Grand Prix at Spa would be on Sunday 25 August, only a week and a half away. (At least one information sheet previewing Spa, with an early deadline, got caught out and had Gachot down among the drivers.)

Jordan Technical Director Gary Anderson remembers 'we were running with de Cesaris, and Gachot was coming down to test. Eddie [who was taking a break in Spain] called on the Tuesday and said "Gachot's court case hasn't quite gone the way we hoped it would. He's being sentenced tomorrow." Eddie called the next morning and said "he's not coming. What are we going to do?" We had this telephone conversation – well, debate – and it ended up with three names: Stefan Johansson, Damon Hill and Michael Schumacher. We weighed one thing and another up. I suggested that Schumacher was the candidate because I thought he knew Spa through sports cars. I'd watched a tape of him winning the International Formula 3 race at Macau the year before and I thought he looked pretty handy. I said "so why don't we give it to the new guy?" Damon Hill was driving for Middlebridge in Formula 3000 and it was pretty hard to warm your heart to Damon.

*Poise in qualifying.
This poise made
a deep impression
on all who*
*witnessed it, and
made them
wonder what the
kid could do.*

I don't know why. It always was difficult and in 3000 he wasn't anything exciting. Johansson [who'd been around since 1983] was a known quantity.'

Anderson's personal philosophy led him to recommend hiring Schumacher. 'It was what you should be doing: get rid of the dead wood, get in some new guys.' What is the point, Anderson muses, of hiring people who've had a chance of beating the front runners and not done it? You might as well hire the new guys who, all else aside, just could be able to do it.

Schumacher's manager Willi Weber had been pounding Eddie Jordan in Spain by phone, saying how quick Schumacher was – 'bloody quick!' Naturally Jordan wanted assurance that Schumacher had already driven Spa, most fearsome of the Formula 1 circuits, and Weber said Schumacher had driven it 'I think about 100 times!'[3] Jordan stalled for time but Weber maintained the pounding, ringing every hour.

In fact, the Jordan team had cast their net wide. Ian Phillips, the Commercial Manager and a very experienced operator in Grand Prix racing, had 'spent ages talking with Keke Rosberg and Derek Warwick in particular and a little bit to Stefan Johansson about doing the race at Spa.'

Eddie Jordan rang Trevor Foster, the Team Manager, sounding him out. Foster had noted what Schumacher did at Sugo in that Formula 3000 race and knew how difficult it was to do well in Japan. Eddie Jordan, however, was anxious to have Rosberg for reasons of credibility. The Jordan team was in its first season of Formula 1, had only about 30 employees and very little money. Rosberg, a tremendous presence as well as World Champion in 1982, certainly represented credibility. Schumacher, Jordan pointed out, lacked any Formula 1 experience at all.

Yes, Foster said, but Rosberg's 43.

'Is he?' said Jordan. 'I thought he was only about 38!' Jordan's personal preference was Johansson, who could be relied on to do a solid, professional job, but – and years later Jordan would wonder at the passage of time and the

The start at Spa, Schumacher is already up with Gerhard Berger (McLaren) from the fourth row at La Source hairpin. He wouldn't get much further.

change in his circumstances – this August 1991 he thought in terms of survival and Mercedes were backing Schumacher. Mercedes were many things, but not poor.

Whenever Jordan put the phone down, as it must have seemed, it rang again: Weber. . . .

A deal was struck. Weber would pay £80,000 for Schumacher to test the Jordan at Silverstone the following Tuesday, three days before the Belgian Grand Prix meeting began, and after the test Jordan could decide what they wanted. The Monza test finished with de Cesaris fifth quickest overall (1:24.91 against Nigel Mansell in the Williams, 1:22.55).

That weekend Schumacher, partnering Karl Wendlinger, competed in the World Sports Car Championship round at the Nürburgring but the engine failed after ten laps, although in qualifying he had crashed into Derek Warwick's Jaguar.

Warwick remembers the whole episode vividly. 'It was two weeks after the death of my little brother[4] and it was my first race since that. It was obviously a very emotional weekend for me. I was quickest, then Schuey took the pole off me, then I took the pole back off him, then he took the pole off me again. I went back out with new tyres and he had finished his lap: we'd timed it so that we knew he'd finished – but because he was at the Nürburgring he was doing a second lap on his qualifying tyres, basically playing to the crowd. He reached me [Warwick on a slow out-lap] about two thirds of the way round the circuit. I saw him coming, tried to get right out of his way – up on the kerbs. When we got out the other side of the corner, and remember we're doing over 100 miles an hour, he drove straight into the front end of my car taking off the left-hand corner.

'He drove back to the pits. I was, and it's an understatement, absolutely furious. I was on the limiter, I really was. I drove flat out directly into the pits on three wheels, didn't stop at my pit, I stopped at Mercedes. I got out of the car when it was still running to a halt. I can laugh now – but I was taking my helmet off, throwing my helmet down before I even got into the Mercedes pit. As I went in – I didn't know who the driver had been, all I knew

was that it had been a Sauber[5] – and there was Jean-Louis Schlesser[6] sat on a toolbox just taking off his crash helmet. As he's taking it off I've cocked my arm and I'm about to hit him because I thought it was him.'

Schlesser said 'what do you want, Derek?'

'You pushed me off.'

Warwick remembers Schlesser replying 'no-no-no, not me, Schumacher!'

As Schlesser points out, 'Mercedes had two cars, I was with Jochen Mass in one and I didn't push anybody off.'

'I turned round,' Warwick says, 'and Schumacher was running out through the back of the garage. I gave chase.'

Schlesser remembers 'Warwick running after him!'

'We went through one transporter back into another and he tried to lock himself into the physio room of one of the Sauber transporters,' Warwick says. 'I forced my way in and it all started getting a little bit ugly. Over one shoulder I've got Schlesser' – and, Warwick says, Schlesser was urging him to explain the facts of life to Schumacher. And, Warwick adds, 'that's his team-mate, remember!'

Schlesser remembers Warwick 'talking very strongly' to Schumacher, saying 'you should not do this.' It was, concludes Schlesser, 'the old story, driver against driver.'

'Then,' says Warwick, 'Mr Nice Guy – Jochen Mass –

calmed it all down. By this time we had photographers and TV crews and Jaguar mechanics and Sauber mechanics all in this little physio room.

'There are two things you must say. One is that I was emotionally charged because of the circumstances. He was young and aggressive. I am Michael Schumacher's biggest fan by a country mile, let me tell you. The biggest thing that let him down, to me, was the fact that he never really apologised although he was forced to by the ADAC[7] next day. He didn't ever really apologise and he must have been aware of my circumstances and the only thing I can say is that I won the race.'

FISA reprimanded him for 'misbehaviour and dangerous practice'.

Hey, I'm a Grand Prix driver now and it's great. . . The change-over: Schumacher joins Benetton for the Italian Grand Prix, the race after Spa, and gets to meet Flavio Briatore, who is running the team.

That Sunday night Phillips 'got a call from Eddie saying "I've done a deal with Michael Schumacher." I had to phone these other blokes, Rosberg and so on, to explain that Schumacher had got the drive and they all said "who?"'

Warwick accepts that there was an irony in the man who had crashed him at the Nürburgring taking the Jordan drive away, 'but that's life. Michael had some sponsorship and he had Mercedes behind him. And, as history proves, Jordan made the right decision. Incidentally, I always remember driving against Schumacher in sports cars – you know, the hour stint you do – but I can't even remember ever driving against Frentzen or Wendlinger or Fritz Kreutzpointner.[8] That guy Schumacher, even in those days, was looking special.'

Weber, Neerpasch and Schumacher travelled to England and visited the Arrows team [at that time named Footwork] at Milton Keynes, then moved on to the Jordan factory at Silverstone some 20 miles away. That was the Tuesday and, as Foster says, 'it was the only chance we had to do a seat fitting – remember we had very limited resources in those days, a very limited number of [Cosworth] engines.' Foster fretted that if Schumacher broke an engine during the test that would be one engine less for Spa. 'We couldn't go to Cosworth and say "well,

here's another £30,000, can we have a fresh engine" because we didn't have it.'

The seat fitting completed, Schumacher came into the workshop and 'sat down on a bench,' Anderson says. 'His English was already pretty good. He wanted to know how he should drive the car, wanted to know what were the good parts of the car and what were the bad parts – because there is no point in exploiting the bad bits rather than try to exploit the good bits. Before he drove the car you knew that he was thinking like that, his mind was saying to him: *there is no point in trying to drive the bad bits*. I saw it again when he joined Ferrari and initially their car wasn't that good, but he won races with the good bits, leaving the bad bits alone.'

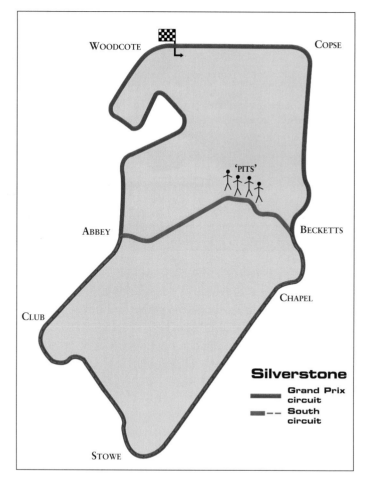

On this Tuesday, however, Schumacher – utterly without experience and facing a decisive moment in his life trying to master a vehicle of enormous complexity and power – was asking the Technical Director what was wrong with the Technical Director's own creation.

'But it's the right way to do it,' Anderson insists. 'We've had so many drivers through the years that I've been involved with and, let's say, they come from Williams. They drive the car and they want to make it a Williams – I don't know what a Williams is. You've got what you've got. There is no point spending all your time trying to make it a car it will never be. Michael was just open-minded.'

They went across to the South Circuit at Silverstone – Anderson, Foster, Phillips and three mechanics – where, with Weber watching, Schumacher prepared to drive a Formula 1 car for the first time. Foster remembers that Schumacher was 'very cool, very calm' although he'd been told that the car was his race car which, after the test, would go straight onto the transporter for Spa. The imperative was not to damage it in any way, especially the engine. With a manual gearchange, as Jordan had then, over-revving was perilously easy and if that happened Cosworth would insist – no argument – that the engine came out. In both senses, the literal and financial, Jordan could not afford this.

Schumacher said 'yeah'.

He went out with Foster's words still ringing in his ears:

this is the race car, this is the race engine, don't . . .

Anderson re-iterates what Foster has said. 'You could over-rev it very easily because it had a stick gearchange – but with the sports car experience that he had had, that was probably one of the least of his problems. He came from a background where you weren't allowed mistakes like that. In a 24-hour sports car race or a 6-hour sports car race, you can't do things like that. As far as car respect was concerned, he had that already, had it as good as anybody.'

The vivid-green Jordan moved onto the South Circuit. 'You *knew* immediately,' Anderson says. 'The car control, the finesse, was just . . . he was the master, no problem.'

That does not alter the fact that on his opening lap, as Schumacher approached where the little group were standing, they all thought *bloody hell, that's quick* and retreated.

'We stepped back,' Anderson says, ' because all we had was just a bit of barrier, and the track was bloody quick there, probably 150, 160 miles an hour before you braked for the chicane – and first time round, approaching us, he was going a bit quick, and with him being new you thought *oooops*. Having said that, and taking nothing away from him, the 1991 car was a good car to drive, not for being fastest but for being good to the driver.'

Phillips describes the South Circuit as 'very frightening. You stood against a bit of Armco barrier and the ordinary blokes would brake before they got to the kink leading to the chicane. Michael came past us still flat out. . . .'

'He was one of these guys who thinks of everything that's going on,' Anderson says. 'His approach is about driving the car and understanding what he's doing. It's very easy to over-drive a car. If the car is two-tenths off the pace you can make it half a second off the pace because you are over-driving it. But if you take the best out of it, you'll only be the two tenths off. The sports car was good experience for him in terms of pure speed and miles: you do mile after mile after mile. And you have to drive a sports car when it's not right – a sports car is never right![9] You've either got confidence in your ability or you don't have. And it's better to drive a car on the limit, and accept you are able to do that, rather than wait all the time to try and go quick. You're not going to feel confident doing that, are you?'

Foster watched as Schumacher had the brakes glowing in the chicane. Foster watched as he flicked the Jordan through. Foster turned to Weber and said they'd got to bring Schumacher in and 'slow him down by getting him out of the car!'

At Spa with the Jordan for the Belgian Grand Prix, curious about everything. . . . Listening to the wise counsel of Trevor Foster.

'After three laps,' Phillips says, 'Trevor turned round to Weber and said "I'm going to call him in, he's going too quick" and then he said to me "go and phone Eddie and tell him we've found a star." So I went off to do that.'

Schumacher seemed not to understand this fuss. As Anderson says, 'well, he wouldn't. He had that confidence, he knew what he was doing. He wasn't a new boy, it was just a new problem. He went out for a run and we brought him in because he *was* going too quick. That first lap we stepped back, second lap he went a little bit wide, third lap I think we brought him in.'

Schumacher found these first three laps 'quite impressive' in the sense of the impression they made on him, but thereafter the experience softened into normality. He could do it.

They reminded him it was the race car, and it was all they had.

'Fine,' he said.

They got Weber to remind him. Weber did and reported that Schumacher didn't understand the problem because there wasn't one.

'In total we did about ten laps and for sure I was forming the impression that he was something special,' Anderson says. 'He did another four or five laps, I must admit a little bit easier but not *intensively* easier because, I think, he wanted to learn a little bit more about gear changes and have the time to think about it all.' Mind you, on one of those he got down to a lap of 54.8 seconds, and that was only 0.4 of a second slower than Jordan's record round the South Circuit.[10]

'By the time I'd phoned Eddie,' Phillips says, 'Michael had been out again and Trevor was calling him in yet again to slow him down!'

The test completed, and with Foster making triumphal noises down the phone to Eddie Jordan in Spain, a price was agreed for Schumacher to drive in the Belgian Grand Prix. It was £150,000. Then Schumacher and Weber returned to Germany.

They arrived at Spa on the Thursday, Schumacher driving them there in his Mercedes 230 Coupé with, in the boot, a fold-up bicycle, and thereby hangs a tale. Despite what Weber told Jordan, Schumacher had never raced at Spa before and had no first-hand knowledge of the imperious and daunting circuit at all. If necessary, he would learn it by riding round on the bike.

In 1985, and driving for Lotus, Ayrton Senna had arrived at Spa a day early because he had never raced there: he entered Grand Prix racing the year before, when the race was at Zolder. Now, alone, he walked and jogged the circuit looking, calculating, remembering. I mention this because one theme of this book is an examination of greatness, and that inevitably involves a comparison between Senna and Schumacher. That both thought ahead when they confronted Spa, and in almost exactly the same way, is very interesting.

Weber and Schumacher had discussed Weber's ploy of claiming he'd driven it hundreds of times and, in view of the fact that he'd never even seen the place before, Weber would have to confess all. Weber said it was all a mix up and he really meant Zolder! [Schumacher had driven Zolder three times in 1988 in Formula Koenig.]

'You bastard!' quoth Jordan, smartly followed by wondering what to do.

Nothing, Weber said. Weber was very, very right.

De Cesaris had promised to give Schumacher a run round the circuit in a road car to point out braking points and so on but he was locked in discussion with Eddie Jordan about a contract for the following season, and that dragged on to the point where Foster had to tell Schumacher sorry, it wouldn't be happening. Schumacher said it wasn't a problem, he had the bike expressly for this, and set off on it. What impressed Foster was that Schumacher didn't ask to borrow a bicycle, didn't ask for a scooter, didn't even ask for a hire car. He'd thought ahead, asked himself what he was likely to need, and stowed the bike in the Mercedes' boot. (To be fair to de Cesaris, he did at least talk Schumacher round a lap, explaining which gears you needed for which corners.)

That evening Weber and Schumacher discovered no hotel had been booked for them but found a room in a youth hostel with two small beds and a toilet between them.

Spa is daunting – the downhill-uphill *Eau Rouge* is regarded within Formula 1 as a yardstick for both men and machines. Mostly the question is whether the driver has the bravery to take *Eau Rouge* flat out.

How did Gary Anderson, who now had a driver with a mere ten laps experience of a Grand Prix car and no experience of Spa, approach all this? 'We hoped at that stage he would just go along at the back of Andrea but he led Andrea from the minute he got in the car. He was in control of what he wanted to do and how he wanted to do it. Andrea wasn't happy with it, he was not a happy camper at all. I am saying that Michael has natural talent and he was able to apply that natural talent without making mistakes because of the sports car experience.

'I didn't have any qualms because you have to give people self respect. It's like standing at the top of a ski slope and saying to the young racer "watch you don't fall over." You don't do that. So at Spa you give a Schumacher or whoever the self respect that they know the levels they can operate at, and if they don't they are never going to make it anyway. You say "welcome to Formula 1."'

Anderson introduces an intriguing point that turns the external perception of racing upside down. 'Your safety cushion gets bigger the faster you go. In a 60kph corner you might try and spin the wheels and slide and stuff, in a 280kph corner you think about it and you respect it. The Bus Stop at Spa – that's where Michael made a mistake that weekend, but not *Eau Rouge*. There are places where you think "I'll have a go, maybe make up a bit of time" but *Eau Rouge* can bite you. The Bus Stop won't.'

Next morning Schumacher ventured onto Spa in the racing car in the untimed session (which would last from 10.0 to 11.30), completed a slow lap moving towards the pace, did 2:12.382 and pitted. Foster asked him how the car was and Schumacher explained where he had understeer and where he had oversteer. Foster earnestly inquired if he was driving over the limit and Schumacher replied affably that he was on it but not over it. On his second run he went quicker and quicker.

Lap 4 2:04.074
Lap 5 2:00.930
Lap 6 1:59.885
Lap 7 2:00.930
Lap 8 1:59.254

Then he pitted again.

De Cesaris, who'd been driving Spa in a Grand Prix car

since 1983, had done a 1:57.965 by his sixth lap. Schumacher made three more runs, the last of them – the eighteenth – a 1:55.322. De Cesaris finished on 1:54.794. Berger (McLaren) was quickest with a 1:50.343, de Cesaris eighth, Schumacher eleventh. On one of these runs he encountered Alain Prost in the Ferrari.

'It was coming in to the Bus Stop,' Ian Phillips says, 'and there was an incident between Michael and Prost. I think Michael forced Prost to take the escape road and sure enough he got summoned to see the Stewards. I went with him' – this was after the untimed session but before first qualifying began at 1.0 – 'and John Corsmit [an experienced FISA official] said "young man, what do you think you were doing?" Michael just said "he was in my way – and he wasn't fast enough." Corsmit was wagging his finger as if to say *behave yourself, I don't want to see you in here again*.'

Gary Anderson remembers that *Blanchimont*, the ultra fast curve before the Bus Stop chicane, had

Mighty Monza and Schumacher moving to a fifth place finish, getting points in only his second Grand Prix.

'just been re-surfaced and that created a bump. Andrea came straight to the pits. He'd tried to go flat out through there and couldn't make it. Something was the matter with the car, he said. We spent the whole bloody Friday trying to find something wrong with the back of Andrea's car. Michael was out there driving the car, getting up to speed. Andrea said "you can't get through *Blanchimont* flat – no way, there's a big bump – but it was flat last year."'

When Schumacher came in he told Anderson 'no-no-no-no, it is flat' and this, concludes Anderson, 'was an experienced guy against an inexperienced guy. At one point Michael said "I'd like to try and fix the understeer a little bit," because the car had a good rear end but it did have understeer. We told him that. We worked on it and that made the understeer better but not the rear end. He went out, did a couple of laps and said "you're right." Was I surprised that someone with lack of experience would raise a matter like that? I don't think from the first second he sat in the car that he thought this driving of a Formula 1 car was ahead of him, he was always ahead of the car. He was never playing catch up. You see him in qualifying now and

he's two corners ahead of the car, some of them are two corners behind it!'

In first qualifying, on what was now a hot and sunny day, Schumacher did two exploratory laps. His third run consisted of a lap out of the pits and then the hot one: 1:53.290. De Cesaris did 1:54.186. Schumacher's astonishing performance made him eighth quickest, something not very far away from a genuine sensation. There was more to it than that.

Anderson asked him if he'd been taking *Eau Rouge* flat and he said 'ah, no, I was making sure everything was OK. I'll be flat tomorrow.' Schumacher, Anderson insists, 'had the self-assurance to say he was working it out, and "when I have done that I will take it flat."'

In the de-brief, de Cesaris went on about the bump at *Blanchimont* and how it was no longer possible to take it flat, while Schumacher sat in silence. Foster was curious if he'd had the same problem as de Cesaris and he said, yes he had for the first couple of laps but lifting off disturbed the balance of the car so he'd been left-foot braking.[11] Schumacher had thought this so obvious a thing to do that it was barely worth mentioning. 'Andrea,' Foster says, 'didn't know that at all.'

That evening Schumacher and Weber, according to Adam Cooper [*Autosport*], ate in a pizzaria in Spa, Schumacher unrecognised, while de Cesaris socialised with Riccardo Patrese (Williams) elsewhere. The point is that next morning de Cesaris reported to Anderson that *Blanchimont* was in fact flat. 'It's OK because Patrese says it's OK.' Anderson ruminates that Schumacher didn't need Patrese or anybody else to tell him what was and wasn't OK – already.

In the Saturday morning untimed session, Schumacher did an immediate 1:58.224 and, as Anderson says, 'first time out, downhill flat, never lifted through *Eau Rouge*. He had the confidence not to do it flat out, and the confidence to do it flat out. Andrea took until the last lap of qualifying before he did it. Every time he'd say "I've done it," we'd get the data out and see a little lift. "You didn't." "I did." "You didn't."'

Schumacher was fastest of all for much of the session,

and used the hour and a half to do 26 laps. He finished fifth, and seventh in second qualifying. His 1:51.212 put him on the fourth row of the grid just behind Nelson Piquet (Benetton) on 1:50.540. In the tight corners he held the Jordan beautifully balanced and was flicking it through with the ease he'd shown at the chicane on the South Circuit.

Reflecting years later, Schumacher would say 'when I knew that I would be driving, I thought I would be around the middle of the grid. In qualifying it was better than that, I was seventh, but I didn't deduce big things. It wasn't until the next race, Monza with Benetton, that I was able to achieve the rhythm of certain of the big names of Formula 1, those who represented something for me and who I had thought were inaccessible. There [at Monza] I said to myself "oops, that's happened better than I thought."'

At the time, however, Anderson says 'the biggest thing he was disappointed about was qualifying seventh and not beating Piquet, who was sixth. I am sure at that point the Benetton thing was hanging in the wind or in talks or whatever.[12] To beat Piquet was a big thing for him.'

But Piquet was three times World Champion.

'Oh yeah, but to him Piquet was only a bloke. That was his biggest upset. He said to me after qualifying "I wanted to be ahead of Piquet."' Piquet, of course, was in the Benetton and if Anderson is correct, beating him would powerfully reinforce any attempt by Schumacher to get into the team himself.

Is that not an extraordinary wish for a young man at his first Grand Prix meeting?

'Obviously you said to him "look, you haven't done too badly," but he said "oh, no, no, no." On his last lap I think he had traffic and if he hadn't he'd have been third or fourth on the grid.'

Schumacher gets a corner wrong on the Thursday before the 1991 Spanish Grand Prix as the drivers explore the new track at Barcelona. . . . Australia that year was chaotic. Schumacher crashed on the Friday (pictured) in the dry and again in the race in the wet.

The Sunday morning warm-up seemed to confirm that because, with the car in race trim, he did a couple of exploratory laps and then settled to a long run working down to 1:56.986 and covering another couple of laps slightly slower before he was satisfied. This increased the general astonishment because the session finished:

Patrese	1:55.211
Mansell	1:55.392
Senna	1:56.752
Schumacher	1:56.986
De Cesaris	1:57.055
Piquet (9th)	1:57.612

When the Grand Prix began he thrust the Jordan to mid-track and was immediately fifth. He dug smoke from his tyres braking into *La Source* hairpin and, in the jostle going round it, lost a place. He ran sixth but in the bowels of *Eau Rouge* the clutch broke. Up at the top he found a gap in the Armco and drove the car slowly through, then parked it. 'He was let down in the race by the clutch,' Gary Anderson says. 'A bit of inexperience on his behalf made that happen, a bit of under-finance on our behalf made that happen. He was down a touch afterwards.'

According to Adam Cooper, Weber and Schumacher set off to their youth hostel to pick up Weber's luggage but, returning to the circuit to get Schumacher's from the Jordan truck, found the roads were all one-way to help get the traffic away from the circuit. They made it, as Cooper says, by doing some cross-country motoring. They didn't mind in the least. They must have known everything had changed forever. They were right.

NOTES

[1] I pay my dues to Adam Cooper's excellent reconstruction of the weekend (*Autosport*, 30 August 2001).

[2] In fact both drives became vacant, and went to de Cesaris and Olivier Grouillard.

[3] Cooper in *Autosport*.

[4] Paul Warwick had been killed at a Formula 3000 race at Oulton Park on 21 July.

[5] The Mercedes cars were run by Swiss team Sauber but were to all intents and purposes works entries.

[6] In 1991, Sauber ran two cars: Jean-Louis Schlesser and Jochen Mass were in one, Schumacher and Karl Wendlinger in the other.

[7] The ADAC, the German Automobile Club, is the equivalent to Britain's RAC.

[8] Fritz Kreutzpointner was a German driver who had made his sports car début at Le Mans in June 1991.

[9] Anderson is sure that the skill of overcoming problems and continuing at high speed across the broad acres of a sports car race – the Le Mans 24-hour race is exactly that – was what helped Schumacher finish second in the 1994 Spanish Grand Prix despite his Benetton being stuck in fifth gear. See Chapter Four: Facts of the matter. 'In sports cars it's about survival, really,' Anderson concludes. Grand Prix cars are so highly stressed for what is essentially a sprint that any little problem can cripple them; sports cars run to an even pace, are highly robust and can be coaxed and nursed to the finish.

[10] Nigel Stepney of Ferrari says that sometimes when they've told Schumacher over the radio to slow down he ends up going faster because, by slowing, he becomes smoother and that saves time.

[11] Left-foot braking is a rally drivers' technique, enabling the driver to keep full power on – preserving the balance of the car – with his right foot at the same time.

[12] Schumacher was snapped up by Benetton immediately after the Belgian Grand Prix in circumstances which are still, perhaps, unclear and controversial.

Facts of the matter

Schumacher drove in the World Sports Car Championship for Mercedes for two seasons. In 1990 he made his début at Silverstone, or rather ought to have done. In the Saturday untimed session the car broke down out on the circuit, the mechanics worked on it there to get it back and he was excluded for work done 'outside the pits'. He did make his début at Dijon (partnering Mass) and they were second to the other Mercedes (Schlesser, Mauro Baldi). They followed with another second at Nürburgring, and a win in the final round in Mexico City when the Schlesser-Baldi car was disqualified for a fuel infringement.

In 1991, after retirements at Suzuka and Monza, Schumacher and Wendlinger finished second at Silverstone, fifth at Le Mans, retired at the Nürburgring, retired at Magny-Cours (he had joined Benetton in Formula 1 by then) and Mexico, won at Autopolis, Japan, the final race of the season and his final race in sports cars.

Schlesser lists Schumacher's team-mates at Mercedes, points out that he never partnered him and says 'I was always in front of him anyway!'

The common language of the team was English. 'It was much easier because our team was like a melting pot. We had people from Austria, from England, from France, from Italy, everywhere, so the basic language was English – except when Schumacher was talking with his engineer, who was German.

'I think as a driver he is exceptional. The domination of a driver always belongs to the head. For me the best example is Jackie Stewart. His head was driving all his career and he put his driving ability at the disposal of his brains. You can see that in his career, which was so fantastic. Then he decided to stop, and he stopped. Sometimes you have a talented driver and he has only talent and he wins occasionally. But if you always see the same people winning in different events and categories they have something more. I think Schumacher wins races because he is cleverer.

'At Mercedes at this time it was very hard for him to accept the domination of me, for example. [In 1990 Schlesser and Baldi were joint World Champions, in 1991 Schlesser was joint seventh, Schumacher joint ninth.] In fact, because he wanted to be in front, he listened to everything. He would go out with the car and attack straight away. He had something more, for sure. There is no doubt about that. It is the same today with Ferrari. He has no weaknesses.'

Chapter Three

DECISIVE BATTLES (2): SPA, 1992

'The first time I came into contact with Michael was at the end of 1991,' Pat Symonds will say quietly, drifting back to those years when he was Schumacher's race engineer and at the very centre of momentous movement from 1992 to 1995.

'I'd been at Benetton for many years and, at the end of 1990, I left and we tried to start Reynard in Formula 1, which folded in about a year.[1] I came back to Benetton at the end of the season and, of course, Michael had already done a couple of races' – the début with Jordan at Spa, the début with Benetton at Monza the race after.

'My first real contact with him was at a test shortly after Monza although, having said that, I did meet him at Reynard when we were looking around at drivers. Adrian [Reynard] brought him along to the factory – this would have been early in that year. I didn't actually know a great deal about him at the time. He was driving for Mercedes and to be honest I don't think he particularly stood out. There was that gang of them: Michael, Wendlinger, Frentzen. I wouldn't have said that, from his sports car career, he really shone but I also believe that that is a fantastic training ground. It teaches the drivers discipline, teaches them to read the race, teaches them to look after their cars.

'In the Monza testing I immediately realised I was dealing with someone special. An engineer assesses a driver, I guess, two ways. Forget about lap times because that's easy for

The first step towards the world record number of wins, Spa 1992, with Nigel Mansell (back to camera) looking pleased. Riccardo Patrese is behind.

anyone to do. The engineer does it by the verbal feedback – the understanding of the car and the situations – and looking at telemetry. You can tell quite a bit about the driver from that data: throttle control, smoothness and so on. He had all that.

'We move into 1992 and, yes, I did think he was going to win a Grand Prix. At the beginning of that year our car wasn't a great one. In fact it was the 1991 car because Rory [Byrne], myself and various other people had come back to Benetton, and were doing a true '92 car. We had managed to do a little bit of work on the '91 car and it was reasonably competitive but we were looking forward to the true '92 car.'

The season began in South Africa (Schumacher 4th) and already its shape was evident. Nigel Mansell and Riccardo Patrese (Williams) were going to be strong, Ayrton Senna (McLaren) was a lurking presence in a disappointing car, Gerhard Berger in the other McLaren was capable of disturbing the form, Jean Alesi (Ferrari) was capable of anything. Schumacher found himself in against strong, experienced runners and so did Martin Brundle, partnering him at Benetton.

'I got on very well with him, I liked him a lot and I think we had mutual respect,' Symonds says. 'I think that you have to earn respect. Friendship is a slightly different thing, it's either there or it isn't. We had a friendship right from the start. Michael was quite opinionated for a guy who was new to the business. He wasn't afraid to say what he thought. I think it's a very good sign. We're talking top line, best in the world here. There's no room for people who aren't dedicated and they have to know their own minds.

'Motor racing is a team business and I think it was illustrated quite well. We were at Kyalami. I can't remember whether we were testing or whether it was the first race that year, but anyway we were running round Kyalami and Michael had a problem, essentially with the car oversteering in the quick corners. For various reasons we were in a position where we couldn't really trim this particular problem aerodynamically. We had to tackle it mechanically

and I looked at the problem and I could understand straight away what it was' – a technical difficulty with the rear suspension. Symonds decided the solution was slightly stiffer rear springs. 'Michael didn't agree. He was thinking of it in very simplistic terms, thinking it would oversteer more. I said "no, just trust me" and we did it and it cured the problem instantly. I think that was a bit of a turning point. He said "OK, this guy knows what he's talking about." From that point on, we had the respect.'

The season unfolded like this: Mexico third, Brazil third. The new car was available at Barcelona. Schumacher finished second.

'I felt we were in a position to win with that,' Symonds says. 'I had high hopes for the car although I can't say to you that I thought we were going to win this race or that race. What I did feel was that, maybe with a little bit of luck, we were in with a chance of a win – because we weren't absolute front-runners.'[2]

After Barcelona, it unfolded as San Marino did not finish, suspension; Monaco fourth; Canada second; France accident; Britain fourth; Germany third; Hungary dnf, suspension failure causing a spin. And then they came to Belgium.

Other than the six circuits he saw the year before, virtually all the tracks were new to him. He had driven Hockenheim in junior formulae single-seaters, Mexico and Silverstone in sports cars in 1990. The rest he didn't know.

'He was still learning it but, you know, the really good drivers don't take long to learn a track,' Symonds says. 'I think most of the drivers will learn 95% of what there is to know in ten laps. The very good drivers will probably get to 98, 99% in ten laps. Getting the further one or two per cent maybe takes them a few years, but Michael was there very, very quickly.

'One of the things to remember is you don't get to the very, very top level – and with Michael we're talking about the very top level, not the Premier division but the top of the Premier division – by being good at one thing. I'd also argue that you don't get there unless you're intelligent. Michael is a very bright man, not necessarily in the academic sense – although he's no fool in that – but he does

have a high intelligence which manifests itself in so many ways, like the ability to recognise what's important and an attention to detail.

'You have to be in the right place at the right time and that's not always luck, in fact it's very rarely luck, it's normally the intelligence to see what's going on. If Michael had found himself in a Minardi he would make it go quicker than anybody thought it could go and *he'd make sure people saw*. He would do the things that matter. I think his natural intelligence plays a larger part in his career.

'To my mind he was the first driver who really appreciated the value of fitness, and not just appreciated it – because all the drivers train – but applied science to it. For example, when we were testing he took it to another level. The basis probably came from Mercedes and what he learned there. If we were doing a race distance we'd stop half way for tyres or something, and we'd take a blood sample from him. His trainer, a good guy, would analyse that and make sure when he was training he'd get a similar blood analysis. Don't ask me the technicalities, but it ensured that his training was fitted to the aerobic rates of driving a racing car on the pace. *That's* the sort of thing that made him different.'

The moods of 1992 . . . fourth at Monaco, his first Grand Prix there.

Symonds, however, adds an intriguing insight. 'His weak point was when he wasn't flat out. In those early days in 1992, we had a manual gearbox and he was dreadful at over-revving engines on an "out" or "in" lap. When he was driving at racing speed everything was fine, everything was very precise, but he damaged a lot of engines coming in and out because he didn't have that rhythm, or rather his rhythm had been broken.'

This was the young man who arrived at Spa on the Thursday for what would be his eighteenth Grand Prix. Schumacher said he had 'a funny sort of feeling. Just as I did in 1991, I rode my bike to the track. I even stayed at the same place and tried to follow a similar routine – but I had a very different feeling about everything. I had a strong impression it might be one of those weekends. . . .'

On the Friday morning he suffered an engine failure, in the afternoon he spun but still finished third. It rained on the Saturday and in the morning untimed session Schumacher went fastest.

Schumacher	2:13.26
Mansell	2:13.97
Berger	2:14.60

Nobody could improve their Friday times in the afternoon (even these men can't do that in the wet) and so Schumacher had qualified on the second row of the grid. Mind you he was evidently going through the *Blanchimont* curve flat[3] and nobody else was doing that.

	Mansell
Senna	
	Schumacher
Patrese	
	Alesi
Berger	

The Sunday morning warm-up (9.30 to 10.0) is arguably more important than qualifying because the cars run in race trim. In it, the weather cool but sunny, Schumacher was second fastest to Mansell. A glimpse of Schumacher: he strides confidently along the corridor between the transporters, shadows falling in wedges across him, and he smiles for the television cameras – a confident smile – and walks swiftly on. At the track Schumacher found that the Benetton, which had been 'good in qualifying', was now 'for some reason better than ever and that filled me with confidence.'

'After the warm-up,' Symonds says, 'there is a de-brief going through the car – very important, because that's your true and final check-up for the race. After that, we try and let the drivers relax as much as possible (the race is at 2.0). Normally on a Sunday morning they do have a little bit of PR work to do in the Paddock Club and so on, then the relaxation. Then, an hour and a half before the pit lane opens, we always have a pre-race briefing and in that we go through everything to do with the race. We explain the strategy in detail, we explain what the critical parts of the race are. We talk through any problems with the circuit, any

specific points there – these days things like where the white lines are for a pit stop. That's with everyone in attendance, all the engineers and senior technicians, so everyone is absolutely up to speed on *exactly* how we are going to tackle the race. Then the drivers get an hour or so to just sit by themselves and contemplate before they go out.'

In the motorhome, as Schumacher waited after the briefing, the 'feelings just got stronger as the race came nearer and nearer. I don't know why. When I was in the motorhome before the race I had it in my mind that I might have my first victory, and the first by a German driver since Jochen Mass in 1975, but I hardly dared to really think hard about it.'

Dark clouds were gathering over Spa and as 2.0 approached, rain fell.

Schumacher moved from the pits to take his place on the grid. The grid is a crowded place, full of mechanics working as if from memory and people who like to be on television and drivers preparing in whatever way they have found suits them best. At Spa, the grid snakes back into the curve from the Bus Stop.

At such moments you might imagine that Michael Schumacher's composure would be so total as to make him cold, because that's what his facial and body language suggested.

'Funnily enough, no,' Symonds says. 'He wasn't excited, his demeanour was calm but he was, I think, always a bit unsure of things. What I mean by that is when he'd go to the grid, he might do a couple of laps out of the pits. That's not a great time to think too much about the car. With the way Grand Prix racing is, you do a warm-up in the morning early on a relatively cool track and nine times out of ten you're going to be dealing with a hotter track in the afternoon. You have to adjust the car accordingly. You know what needs to be done. You look at the track temperatures and you make your assessments of how you're going to alter the balance of the car for the race. You know a bit more about what tyre degradation's going to be like.

'Those couple of laps from the pits to the grid are not always a terribly good indication of what the car's going to do. For instance, it's good for checking ride heights but you're not on perfect tyres because you've kept your best tyres for the race, and depending on how practice has gone you may not be on good tyres at all.[4]

'A lot of drivers come up to the grid and say "it wasn't great on those couple of laps but, you know, it'll be all right." Michael wasn't like that. I think we changed settings on Michael's car on the grid more than any other driver I have ever worked with. He'd say "ah, I'm not quite happy, there's a bit too much understeer." I'd say "all right, we'll come down a little bit on the roll bar."'

It made me wonder if a certain amount of kidology was involved, in the sense that Symonds would pretend to make an adjustment.

'No. I would never do that because I would feel that to be dishonest. Occasionally if I felt he was over-reacting I would make a change to the car that I knew was really trivial: much more a psychological change. I'd never say we'd changed something which we hadn't. That would destroy the trust. If I felt – and you know I could read him – that he really did think that there was a problem we would most certainly react to it, and apply the best knowledge I had. But if I felt it was just a little bit of nerves showing, yes, I'd make a change to the car but one which really wasn't going to make much difference, just to calm his nerves down. His demeanour never showed it, he wasn't shouting in the cockpit. It would be: deep thought, then "I think we should do this, and I think we should do that." To my mind, more often than not it was psychological.'

The rain had eased and all 26 cars would start on dry tyres.

When the green lights went on, Schumacher got lost in the scrambling jostle towards *La Source* hairpin and went round it fifth, two places lost. The immediate order was Senna, Mansell, Patrese, Alesi, Schumacher. In the hustle at *Les Combes*, the right-hander feeding them out into the Ardennes countryside, Schumacher moved inside Alesi and was fourth. As they crossed the line to complete the opening lap, Schumacher had drawn full up to Patrese. The

The moods of 1992 . . . crashing with Senna (McLaren) and later Stefano Modena (Jordan) in France.

rain was harder, the tyres digging wisps of spray. On the long run to the Bus Stop Mansell went past Senna and at the entrance to the Bus Stop, Patrese did too. Schumacher hovered behind Senna and pressured him – a glimpse of past, present, future – while, behind, Brundle was about to move up to fifth. Immediately Mansell and Alesi pitted for wets.

The driver, of course, is not alone. He can speak on the radio and in Schumacher's case that was to Pat Symonds. 'On the parade lap there is nearly always silence – it would be rare to speak. The first few laps of the race, it's quite rare to be speaking too, because it's a high workload for the driver, lots of traffic around and not much you can tell him. Generally the race conversations begin once the race is starting to develop a little bit.'

Mansell emerged fourteenth, Alesi fifteenth as the other 24 moved through lap 4. And Schumacher pitted for wets. Symonds charts the background. 'I doubt that we spoke until we were talking about that tyre change. It would be unlikely. In those conditions the driver's workload is even higher than normal because of the slippery conditions. A couple of people had stopped the lap before, Mansell and Alesi, and I'd have told him that – I'd certainly have told him Alesi had stopped, and he'd have seen Mansell stopping because it was all quite close at the front.'

Schumacher was now ninth, immediately behind Mansell, and the Benetton felt terrific on the wets. Patrese pitted, passing the lead back to Senna who stayed out on *dries*, calculating that his only chance was to hold on in case the rain stopped. Here was an interesting comparison. Senna, the master of the late 1980s and early 1990s, applied his formidable intellect to the problem of Spa this day and concluded that dries were the best tactic. Schumacher, master of the mid to late 1990s and early 2000s, applied his formidable logic to the same problem and pitted immediately for wets. . . .

Ninth caused no concern at Benetton, of course, because as Symonds points out 'there was a flurry of cars coming in, and in fact even on that lap four cars had come in, then the next two laps everyone was piling in. Ayrton stayed out a long while – he didn't come in until lap 14. He'd gambled on the weather changing back but dropped from first to seventh from lap 10 to lap 14. Michael worked his way up to third by lap 13 with Mansell and Patrese in front of him.'

It settled like that although on lap 26 the clouds were departing, luring Thierry Boutsen, a Belgian, to pit for dries. That might have been a moment of revelation for all the others because Boutsen in the Ligier was going well on slicks but a lap later lost it at *Blanchimont* and was out.

On lap 30 at *Stavelot*, the horseshoe before *Blanchimont*, Schumacher 'went wide and off. I missed the apex and when I turned in, it was too late and so I turned wide. I was really lucky not to go into the barrier.' Brundle, of course, moved past him and 'as soon as he got by I could see his tyres were blistered and that was my luck because it helped me make my decision to go immediately for new tyres.'

'Michael made a mistake and spun the car or half spun it,' Symonds says. 'He dropped behind Martin and the great thing was he saw Martin's tyres and thought "they're not looking in a very good state" so he came straight in, and that was an extremely good move. One of our rules of engagement is that only the race engineer speaks to the driver so it would have been me who spoke to him. If the driver wants to go from dry to wet tyres that is totally his decision, if he wants to go from wet to dry tyres he has to have an acknowledgement from the pit because we can read a bit more of the race than he can, by watching television and so on.

'In this particular case we were thinking about dry tyres anyway, that was close. He came on the radio and being Michael he didn't just say "I want dries," he explained exactly what had happened. "I have seen Martin's rears, let's go to dries." I really didn't have to think much, because to me that was an excellent reason, although maybe a lap or two laps earlier than I would have done if it had been entirely my decision. I had no qualms at all. We had this mutual respect and if he made that decision it was because he'd not only seen something, he'd analysed it and he'd also communicated it. Therefore it really wasn't a difficult thing.

The moods of Monza, 1992. . . . the drivers versus the Press and if you look closely you'll see the Press smiling. They realise he can really play. Afterwards he had to talk to the Press – about the Press team's performance? Hope not . . .

'He made his final pit stop on lap 30 and from that point on he just charged, once he was on the new tyres he just absolutely charged and this was his ability to read the race and say "now is the time." That would normally be a communication from the pit to him but very often it'd be unnecessary because he'd realise. He's in third place, he's pitted, he knows the others have to come in at some stage and he knows we are now in a very critical part of the race. We would, however, reinforce that on the radio. "OK, this is where it really counts."'

So Schumacher made his second stop on lap 30, and here it was: the ability he would make famous and feared by suddenly increasing his pace and sustaining it to gain enough time to lead when Mansell and Patrese pitted. In the statistics below, Schumacher was on slicks, but the advantage was there to be taken:

	Mansell	Patrese	Schumacher
Lap 31	2:09.01	2:09.91	2:15.10 *out lap*
Lap 32	2:07.19	2:13.33 *pits*	1:59.82
Lap 33	2:11.18 *pits*	2:17.73 *out lap*	1:58.41
Lap 34	2:10.51 *out lap*	2:01.47	2:00.43

Schumacher led by some six seconds.

This ability, which would reach its consummation with Ross Brawn at Ferrari, 'always surprised' Symonds. 'There are two parts to that. Michael was exceptional at remembering what had happened during a lap. That may sound quite trivial but a lot of drivers are absolutely on the limit, they are using all their mental capacity and if you ask them about the lap afterwards, yes, they'll tell you "sure it understeered at that corner" or "sure it oversteered at that corner." Michael could remember every little detail of it down to the level of where a gearshift was maybe not quite as he expected. There was always that little bit of spare mental capacity. He could be running at a hell of a speed – quicker than anyone else – and you'd look at the strategy and think we actually need a little bit more. You only had to ask him for this and it was there. I have not worked with a driver since him who could really do that, and we've had some pretty good drivers.'

Ten laps remained and Symonds says 'that was the only time I was worried. It did look like we were going to win it and in a situation like that you always think it can only go wrong now. It's difficult for me to say whether he was calm or not, but certainly his driving was perfect. He's the sort of bloke who would get emotional afterwards. During those ten laps I don't think we spoke much on the radio. There might have been the occasional "take it easy" from me – reassurance – but not much conversation. He's going to do it anyway. When he crossed the line [36.59 seconds in front of Mansell] he came straight on and he was just screaming' – with joy.

Schumacher would say 'I have to admit I really did cry after the race. I just felt so very happy.'

Then came the curious sense of anti-climax, something Symonds describes as 'the unfortunate thing about European races. At somewhere like Spa you've got to get out, you've got to get to an airport, there's no time for celebrations. The fly-away races[5] are a lot better because at least you can celebrate your win. At Spa, it was a bit like *right, off to the airport.* We are still very disciplined, we must do our de-briefs – that would be in the motorhome and last about 15 minutes, not terribly long. Michael was there, he had to be. That is immediately before we leave the circuit. It's a shame because then you're fighting your way through the traffic and when finally you do get to the airport you suddenly think *Jeez, OK, we won that race!*'

The need to make these unseemly rushes from circuits has long been a mystery to me, although I suspect there are several reasons. Formula 1 people spend enough nights away in any year, the transporters and motorhomes face long journeys home but, more than that, there is a distrust of sentiment, as if looking back and savouring is somehow a weakness. There's a macho pace within Formula 1 so that the personnel – who use American words like 'guy', 'down to the wire' and 'ballpark figure' because they sound tough – must always be seen to be travelling at great speed to somewhere else.

On the evening of 30 August 1992 this is what happened. Spa emptied. The victory was partially lost within that, as they all are, but even so nobody could doubt that Michael Schumacher would win a lot more races and, from these, championships would logically follow.

NOTES

[1] Reynard Racing Cars, a celebrated UK car maker in the junior formulae (and recipient of the Queen's Award for Export Achievement in 1990), intended to compete in Formula 1 in 1992 but never made it.

[2] Any driver's first win is a profound psychological moment, and not at all easy to achieve. For example Rubens Barrichello, partnering Schumacher at Ferrari from 2001, of course, took 124 races before he did it. The psychological aspect is that afterwards the driver knows he can win again – and again.

[3] But he was taking *Blanchimont* flat in 1991 despite the bump – see the previous chapter.

[4] With the limit on the number of tyres a driver can use over a Grand Prix weekend, the actual usage is of profound tactical importance.

[5] Fly-away is Formula 1 speak for the races which are a long-distance from Europe.

Facts of the matter

The great ones announce themselves early, and the three lists are an exploration of that. Here are how many Grands Prix what we'll call The Famous Five needed to secure their first pole position, first win and first World Championship.

	Pole	Win	Champ
Fangio	2 races	2 races	2 seasons
Moss	21 races	21 races	Never
Clark	16 races	17 races	4 seasons
Senna	16 races	16 races	5 seasons
Schumacher	42 races	18 races	4 seasons

In 1950, the first year of the World Championship, Fangio was already a mature man (aged 39) and had been driving at a genuinely competitive level for a decade. He was in no sense a beginner in 1950 and, as a consequence, did not have to serve an apprenticeship with smaller teams. In Alfa Romeo, he had an utterly dominant car. Schumacher's total of 42 races before his first pole (Monaco 1994) seems strange but the key is in the next column, 18 races to the first win. The Benetton generally lacked the edge in the bomb-burst of speed which qualifying requires, but Schumacher could make it win races. Incidentally, at Monaco that year he said: 'It's the first time I've done a qualifying lap where afterwards I was not able to say I could have found a tenth of a second at some corner. I couldn't go any quicker.'

You can make out a strong case for including the next five drivers among the very greatest.

	Pole	Win	Champ
Ascari	9 races	9 races	3 seasons
Stewart	42 races	8 races	5 seasons
Lauda	30 races	31 races	4 seasons
Prost	21 races	19 races	6 seasons
Piquet	24 races	24 races	3 seasons

Ascari was similar to Fangio in that for him, too, the World Championship started in mid-career.

Now let's put in five modern drivers who won the championship only once.

	Pole	Win	Champ
Rosberg	45 races	49 races	5 seasons
Mansell	52 races	72 races	12 seasons
D Hill	10 races	13 races	4 seasons
J Villeneuve	1 race	4 races	2 seasons
Häkkinen	94 races	96 races	8 seasons

Hill and Villeneuve were in the immensely strong Williams car. Hill drove 48 times after leaving Williams, got no further pole positions and a single win. To the end of 2003, Villeneuve had driven 82 times since Williams with no pole positions and no wins.

Well, what do you make of that? Schumacher, faced with actress Brigitte Nielsen, doesn't quite know – although the Monza tifosi would have known. Corinna, peeking from the doorway, thinks she knows too, and finds it all hilarious.

Chapter Four

CONQUISTADOR

The championships did logically follow, although on the journey to the first of them – 1994 – Schumacher produced a performance in Barcelona which defied credulity to such an extent that sceptics had to be shown print-outs of the telemetry to believe what they had just seen. And on the way to the second – 1995 – he produced a performance at (inevitably) Spa which demonstrated that a genuinely great driver defeats circumstances, they do not defeat him.

Barcelona was itself a strange, strained weekend. Ayrton Senna and Roland Ratzenberger had been killed at Imola only four weeks before. Karl Wendlinger was seriously injured at Monaco only two weeks before. At Barcelona nine teams refused to take part in the Friday morning untimed session. Instead they were locked in discussions with Max Mosley, President of the FIA, over safety. Out on the circuit a surreal chicane, made of two tyre walls, had been set up to slow the cars.

What Formula 1 needed, absolutely needed, was normality – the normality of those good old days, which seemed much more than a month distant, when the talk would be of racing and racers. Michael Schumacher was going to give it to them.

Schumacher qualified on pole, Hill (Williams) alongside him, and took the lead. Hill pitted on lap 19, Schumacher on lap 21 and he retained the lead. Without warning Schumacher was slowing so markedly that Johnny Herbert (Lotus) flowed past. David Coulthard (Williams) caught Schumacher and flowed past too – unlapping himself.

Schumacher's on-board camera caught his plight because, superimposed on the picture, there was a box showing his revs, another showing his acceleration and a circle with a number inside it. This number showed which of the six gears Schumacher was in. Early in the race the numerals had flicked up and down at each gearchange. Now 5 remained constant.

Monaco 1993. Alain Prost (Williams) is already out of shot in the lead, Schumacher chasing him and Senna chasing Schumacher.

'Spain,' Pat Symonds says with wonderful understatement, 'was an interesting thing. He came on the radio saying that the car was stuck in fifth gear and what should he do? It was a hydraulic failure. We had real-time telemetry so we could see what the problem was and it was obvious we couldn't fix it. There was really no point in coming into the pits and trying to do repairs – if you could have stopped the car for half an hour or an hour we might have been able to! I said to him "well, keep going" – he was leading the race – "keep going and let's see what happens."'

Mika Häkkinen (McLaren), who hadn't pitted yet, caught him, flowed past and now led. Hill caught him just before the tyre chicane and ducked through on the inside.

'He did keep going and I seem to remember that the lap after it happened he lost quite a lot of time [on lap 24 he did a 1:31.503, compared to the 1:25s he'd been doing before the pit stop]. Within two laps or maybe three laps he was not exactly up to his previous pace – because Damon overtook him – but he certainly wasn't far off it. What was stunning was the way he learnt in those couple of laps how to make the most of the car. He did say that that had a lot to do with his Mercedes driving experience where they had to save fuel quite often so he knew how to keep your speed up and your revs down.'

The mood of 1993 . . . braking hard at Imola.

Schumacher would confirm that. 'My experience in Group C sportscars helped me in this because I learnt a lot of ways of running differently, of changing my driving style, usually to save fuel. I used that same driving style now and it certainly helped me a lot.'

Symonds remains, I suspect, slightly in awe. 'I think I am right in saying when he was stuck in fifth gear his best time was something like the third best lap of the race.'

It was. He'd set what would prove to be the fastest of all (1:25.155) on lap 18, from

| Häkkinen | 1:25.872 |
| Hill | 1:25.874 |

and, immediately after that, you've have had to place Schumacher's 1:26.171 on lap 40, his seventeenth lap stuck in fifth. Then

| Brundle | 1:26.233 |
| Lehto | 1:26.346 |

'On the straight Michael did have to back off and that's where most of his lost lap time was,' Symonds says. 'It wasn't actually in the corners.' He could not of course risk maximum revs without sixth gear on that straight. 'The engine was very good, the engine was very tractable and that helped. This was the V8, and it was a good engine.' In those corners Schumacher searched out and found a good line.

He ran second to Hill and, astonishingly, when Hill made his second stop led again, albeit only to his own stop five laps later.

'We even made a pit stop,' Symonds says, 'because we had to stop for fuel and tyres! We discussed for a couple of laps what procedure we'd take, how we'd go about it. You'd have thought getting away from being stationary could be a problem, but we pushed the car to a bit of speed and took some of the jerk out of it.'

The mechanics pushed it with the ferocity that bobsleigh racers use when they are shoving off but, even so, as Schumacher accelerated away the engine seemed to hesitate for an instant. Then, as he moved down the pit lane, it was gurgling nicely again.

'He was able to think about it, think what's the car going to do and be able to make the stop,' Symonds concludes. 'Altogether it was astonishing, although I think a few people realised because they saw he was *feathering*[1] on the straight – but there weren't many that did, and certainly there were an awful lot who didn't believe it afterwards.'

Jonathan Palmer, former driver and now commentating on the BBC, missed nothing, however, although he shared the incredulity. 'Watching Schumacher leave the pits he certainly, as far as I could tell, did not leave in first gear. He gave it a lot of revs and the car lurched a bit as he moved away. I still find it very hard to believe that he's actually stuck in fifth gear.'

Schumacher finished 24 seconds behind Hill and, in the circumstances, said 'for me it's something like a victory'.

'He took things like mechanical problems pretty well,' Symonds says. 'I mean, off hand I can't recall him ever getting really upset about a car failure. We didn't have a lot, because Benetton have always had extremely high reliability,

but he was quite philosophical about it. The car could go wrong in the same way that he could make a mistake. The thing is he's a team player. There are certainly some drivers around who feel that everything revolves around them and if the car breaks they'll scream at the team. What they don't realise is that the whole team does this for a living, this is our lives and it hurts all of us equally. Michael was always philosophical about it. Spain, yes, it was a shame, we'd lost the race through it and we'd lost four points towards the championship. His attitude was "OK, that's the way it is."'

Symonds gives another example of Schumacher's sheer tenacity, what he calls a 'stunning example'. This was in Canada in 1995 on the journey to his second World Championship. 'We were leading that race by miles and we had a problem with the gearbox.' It was stuck in third. 'Michael came on the radio and said "OK, that's it, all over but I can get back to the pits." He got back to the pits, we managed to re-set the gearbox and he went out again. He'd been leading this race, obviously putting in quicker lap times than anyone else, and now he was nowhere' –

The moods of a test session . . . this one at Estoril. Schumacher plays football, Corinna in goal and the dog in central defence. At a Grand Prix you can eat like a banquet. In testing, you eat where you can.

seventh. 'He drove that car like there was no tomorrow. From that point on, his laps were just so much quicker than anyone else's and he got in the points. *That* is a mark of the great ones.'

As a matter of first principle, they drive as competitively as they can in all circumstances because they are made like that and, tactically, you never know. On lap 62 Gerhard Berger (Ferrari), sixth, made an ill-judged attempt to take Brundle (Ligier), fifth, and they were both out. It meant Schumacher inherited Brundle's position and the two points this brought. Championships have been won and lost on less.

That he finished the Canadian Grand Prix fifth, 44.676 seconds behind the winner, Alesi (Ferrari), was irrelevant.

By Spa in late August (when, incidentally, Schumacher's move from Benetton to Ferrari had been confirmed), he led Hill 56–45. The weather wreaked its havoc, Hill qualifying eighth and Schumacher sixteenth. Symonds, wielding understatement again, describes this as 'interesting'. He explains that 'during qualifying on Saturday it was typical Spa, wet and drying out. Everything depended on one lap right at the end and we had a gearbox problem during qualifying – it started shifting of its own accord and Michael came on the radio and said "I've got a problem." I said "well, we'll finish the lap" – if you don't you're nowhere. He did finish the lap but was only on the eighth row of the grid.

'His attitude afterwards – bearing in mind that he's won the World Championship the year before and he's going for it again – was no hysterics, no throwing his toys out of the

The moods of 1993 ... always plenty to look at in Monaco ... Schumacher sprints back to get team-mate Riccardo Patrese's car for the final moments of qualifying at Silverstone after crashing his own. And yes, in Patrese's car he outqualified Patrese. Tracking Prost for the lead in Portugal (above), where Schumacher eventually took the win and Prost took the World Championship.

pram. In actual fact he was very light-hearted about it. Obviously we are professionals and we put just as much effort into it if we've qualified twentieth as we do when we're on pole. He thought "well, I've a bit more to do than I would have liked, but let's do it."'

Symonds sets out this attitude of mind. 'Michael was very good at working with the engineers in developing the car to get the best possible performance out of it and he'd work hard at that through Friday, through Saturday, but come Sunday he'd say "OK, that's what I've got to drive." He would almost switch his skills then. "This is actually what I have to race a Grand Prix in this afternoon so how can I get the best from it?"'

This is known as the art of the possible.

Crossing the line to complete the opening lap, Hill was up to sixth, Schumacher thirteenth. Into *La Source*, the Benetton wobbling under braking, he lunged inside Rubens Barrichello (Jordan) to be twelfth; Häkkinen spun – eleventh. Crossing the line, Schumacher was tenth (Hill fifth). Lap three – eighth some 8.8 seconds behind the leader, Alesi (Hill still fifth). Alesi pitted, Hill third and Schumacher seventh. Herbert, leading, spun and that let Hill through into second. Schumacher had reduced the gap to the new leader, Coulthard (Williams) to seven seconds. Herbert spun in the Bus Stop, balking Blundell (McLaren) – Schumacher fifth. At lap six, however, the gap to Coulthard was out to 9.4 seconds. Schumacher scythed past Irvine (Jordan) at the entrance to the Bus Stop – fourth. Schumacher set off after Berger and hauled him in, pressured him while, on lap 14, Coulthard toured with a gearbox problem – Hill now leading, Schumacher third.

Hill pitted a lap later, Berger following him so that Schumacher led. It had taken no more than 15 laps. Schumacher pitted on lap 18 and came out in second place. Soon enough the rain began and Hill pitted for wet tyres. Schumacher stayed out on dries.

Symonds has already spoken of the mutual respect between Schumacher and himself and explains that 'there were many instances of it' but adds 'we didn't always agree.

A deceptive study from 1993. Schumacher moves easily past Alain Prost (Williams) – but in qualifying! Damon Hill in the other Williams took pole anyway.

I don't think two strong people ever do. There was a classic case at Spa when we were racing Hill for the championship. Basically Michael was out on dry tyres and Damon came in for wet tyres, which I didn't necessarily think was the correct thing to do. We were leading the race and what we had to do was make sure that we got it right: didn't matter if we were a bit slower as long as we made the right decision. We had a discussion about it on the radio and Michael was pretty adamant he wanted to stay on the dry tyres.'

Out on the circuit Schumacher had Hill directly behind him and in theory Hill ought to have breezed by, but Schumacher demonstrated what someone called ruthlessness as he repeatedly blocked Hill – although to be able to do that with dry tyres on a track surface like ice was breathtaking. Hill was angered by the former and impressed by the latter.

'To me it was a risk assessment situation,' says Symonds. 'That assessment was that if we went onto wet tyres we would win the race, if we stayed on dry tyres and it was the right thing to do, we'd win the race by more – but if we stayed on dry tyres and it was the wrong thing to do, we'd lose the race. So it was absolutely obvious. Normally with the rules of engagement that we run at Benetton, the change from dry to wet tyres is the driver's decision [as we've seen] but in this case I over-ruled it. I said "no, we're going onto wet tyres." We had a bit of a discussion about it until finally – because I thought we were wasting time – I commanded him, if you like, on the radio that he had to come in for wet tyres. In he came and changed to wet tyres."'

He did not lose the lead during this pit stop – the Safety Car was out, and Hill came in too – and he won the race by 19.493 seconds. Afterwards Schumacher said to Symonds, "yes, I could tell from your voice that you meant what you said, and I could also tell that you know how to talk to children!"'

Schumacher joined Ferrari and, although in 1996 he was able to conjure three victories, he needed a formidable team behind him.

NOTE

[1] Feathering, as in applying a light touch to the accelerator pedal rather than pressing it full down for maximum power and speed.

Facts of the matter

As a graphic way of illustrating Schumacher's performance when stuck in fifth gear at Barcelona in 1994, here are his lap times from the TAG-Heuer timing system. They prove, in the cold way statistics do, that he was able to run at virtually the same pace before and after. Remember that the gearbox started to misbehave around lap 23.

Lap 1	1:30.840	Lap 34	1:27.576
Lap 2	1:26.971	Lap 35	1:27.674
Lap 3	1:26.552	Lap 36	1:27.061
Lap 4	1:26.462	Lap 37	1:28.687
Lap 5	1:25.936	Lap 38	1:28.571
Lap 6	1:25.709	Lap 39	1:26.340
Lap 7	1:25.713	Lap 40	1:26.171
Lap 8	1:25.597	Lap 41	1:26.884
Lap 9	1:27.542	Lap 42	1:28.140
Lap 10	1:25.553	Lap 43	1:32.870
Lap 11	1:25.768	Lap 44	1:28.050
Lap 12	1:27.202	Lap 45	1:34.742 *(pit)*
Lap 13	1:25.608	Lap 46	1:52.749
Lap 14	1:27.214	Lap 47	1:27.950
Lap 15	1:25.770	Lap 48	1:27.468
Lap 16	1:26.341	Lap 49	1:27.720
Lap 17	1:25.694	Lap 50	1:28.066
Lap 18	1:25.155	Lap 51	1:27.882
Lap 19	1:26.009	Lap 52	1:27.514
Lap 20	1:27.732	Lap 53	1:26.983
Lap 21	1:37.326 *(pit)*	Lap 54	1:27.202
Lap 22	2:02.829	Lap 55	1:28.802
Lap 23	1:31.835	Lap 56	1:28.803
Lap 24	1:31.503	Lap 57	1:27.896
Lap 25	1:29.368	Lap 58	1:28.297
Lap 26	1:30.282	Lap 59	1:28.873
Lap 27	1:29.634	Lap 60	1:28.853
Lap 28	1:28.438	Lap 61	1:31.903
Lap 29	1:28.740	Lap 62	1:30.877
Lap 30	1:27.970	Lap 63	1:32.240
Lap 31	1:27.129	Lap 64	1:31.417
Lap 32	1:27.277	Lap 65	1:35.387
Lap 33	1:27.193		

The winner, born to it, doing it, loving it (top). This is the aftermath of Belgium 1995. There may be trouble ahead. With Benetton just a memory, Schumacher went all out to win the championship for Ferrari. Here at Jerez in 1997 (above) he handles a Press Conference with rival Jacques Villeneuve. On the track they crashed and there it is on the big screen for all to see (right).

Chapter Five

TIME
TEAM

A question to Jody Scheckter who, for two decades, had a phrase attached to him like a billboard: 'last man to win the World Championship in a Ferrari'.

After 1979, was it necessary for Ferrari to shed some passion and hire pragmatic Anglo-Saxons to win the championship again, because they were competing against pragmatic Anglo-Saxon teams?

'They did, and it was no good for many years.'

This is a reference to Dr Harvey Postlethwaite and John Barnard, who both designed Ferraris which did not win the World Championship. It also introduces the idea that making Ferrari a successful team again was no simple matter, because Postlethwaite and Barnard both knew their business and had had significant successes of their own.

Looking back, it is difficult to comprehend the size of the problems Luca di Montezemolo inherited when he became Ferrari President in November 1991, with a brief to turn round the production car company and the Formula 1 team. He would do more than fulfil his brief. He'd create a culture within the company which, based on absolute excellence, led logically to Schumacher and Hungary and Suzuka in 2001.

Enzo Ferrari died in 1988. Although the team finished second in the Constructors' title that year they slipped to third in 1989 (drivers Nigel Mansell and Gerhard Berger), rallied to second in 1990 (Mansell and Alain Prost), were third again in 1991 (Prost, Jean Alesi, and Gianni Morbidelli). The team looked to be without discipline or direction, possibly beyond salvation except as a wonderful but increasingly irrelevant adornment to Formula 1 racing. As if to emphasise that, Prost – who'd arrived as the saviour – was fired after the 1991 Japanese Grand Prix on 20 October. Morbidelli, a journeyman, replaced him for the

Shooting range in South Africa, 1992.

Australian Grand Prix on 3 November. Di Montezemolo arrived at Maranello 12 days later.

CURRICULUM VITAE: The Marquis Luca Cordero di Montezemolo, born 31 August 1947, Bologna. Studied commercial law in Rome and attended Columbia University, New York. Joined the Lancia rally team, joined Ferrari in 1973. Took the team to championships with Niki Lauda in 1975, 1977. Promoted within the Fiat organisation (which owned Ferrari), becoming managing director of Cinzano, the drinks company, in 1984. From 1985 to 1990 was general manager of the World Soccer Cup held in Italy in 1990. Then Ferrari rang again.

While Ferrari invested some $80 million on re-tooling the production car base, and hiring personnel regardless of nationality, the Formula 1 team sank to fourth in 1992 (Alesi, Ivan Capelli and Nicola Larini) with 21 points against the 164 of Williams. Ferrari did not win a race in 1991 or 1992. Moreover the production cars sold only 2,289 in 1993 – it had been closer to 5,000 in the 1980s – and Ferrari were losing a fortune. Di Montezemolo's revolution would take time.

Screen star, Brazil, 1995 . . . Rory Byrne (left), the quiet man who designed master-pieces . . . Luca di Montezemolo (right), the man who spread out the vision and made it come true.

On 1 July 1993 Ferrari announced that Jean Todt would become Sporting Director, essentially running the Formula 1 effort. He had a background in rallying, and criticism rained down on di Montezemolo's decision to hire him. *Todt is French! Todt doesn't know anything about F1! Todt only knows about rallies!*

That wasn't the point, of course. Todt, a small, neat, fussy man, had worked in the Peugeot organisation where he ran their motorsport and was known as 'can do'. He was organised, understood other modern men, and was once quoted as saying that he 'liked to convince people' that they wanted to work with him. He also understood the mechanisms and nuances of creating and maintaining a team. He had done that with outstanding success in rallying.

CURRICULUM VITAE: Jean Todt, born 25 February 1946, Pierrefort (a tiny place near France's Massif Central). His father was a doctor but Todt wasn't interested in joining a profession – he intended to be a 'great' motorsport champion. It didn't happen. At 20 he was a co-driver (navigator) in rallying and remained active for 15 years. He created Peugeot Talbot Sport to contest World Rallying with the Peugeot 205 Turbo – it won a clutch of titles. He took Peugeot into the World Sports Car Championship but early in 1993 Peugeot made a decision not to manufacture a Formula 1 engine and chassis. Then di Montezemolo rang.

Todt would quickly realise the scale of what faced him, however much he savoured taking it on. He described Ferrari as a 'mythical team' and pointed out that he had loved racing all his life and the fact that he hadn't 'done' Formula 1 only made him more anxious to measure himself against it. In an interview with the *International Herald Tribune* he said there were 'lots of great sides' to his decision.

Years later he'd confess that often enough mighty Ferrari found itself 'fighting with very poor little teams' – reduced in the races to running against those from the back of the grid – and in those days just winning a point was a dream rather than an expectation. In Todt's first full season, 1994 (Alesi, Berger, Larini), they were a distant third in the Constructors' title with three pole positions and a solitary win. At Benetton, young Michael Schumacher was winning the championship with six pole positions and eight wins, although he shared the credit with a South African, Rory Byrne, who supervised the design of the car, and an Englishman, Ross Brawn, who supervised everything else.

Todt did inherit some people you'd need as pillars of any edifice, among them Nigel Stepney who knew exactly what he was doing in the noise, chaos and confusion of the pit lane. I use Stepney as representative of those who, most of them anonymous, are pillars. If you go to any Grand Prix team headquarters you see them peering at computer screens or working in assembly bays. Often they do repetitive jobs.

Stepney was a mechanic and always had been (although he'd wanted to be a footballer). He'd worked with Senna at Lotus and – perhaps there, perhaps everywhere – had evolved a philosophy: *there is no point in being in motor racing, and going to the races, if you have no chance of winning.*

Stepney – solid, genial, experienced – was exactly the kind of man you could use as part of the foundation to construct a team which would win.

CURRICULUM VITAE: Nigel Stepney, born 14 November 1958, Ufton, Warwickshire. Became an apprentice mechanic with a Coventry racing team, Broadspeed, moving to Shadow in Formula 1 in 1979. Elio de Angelis was driving there and when he went to Lotus the following season Stepney went too. He stayed until 1988, joining Benetton and then, in 1991, ran Nelson Piquet's F3000 team. Barnard took him to Maranello in order – no doubt – to bring English pragmatism with him.

In 1993, at Donington, I espied Stepney coming across the paddock on a moped. As he passed me I called out 'is it all true?' and, grinning enormously, he shouted 'yes!' and sped on. I didn't have to specify that I was talking about one aspect of Ferrari which wasn't mythical: the endemic politics and the boiling temperaments. Todt was, though, beginning to bring that under some sort of management structure.

CURRICULUM VITAE: Paolo Martinelli, born 26 September 1952, Modena, Italy. In 1977 got a degree in mechanical engineering from Bologna University and joined Ferrari; then joined the Ferrari Formula 1 department on 'the first day of 1995'. Since then, has worked with engine designer Gilles Simon, widely acknowledged as giving the Ferrari cars power and reliability.

In 1995, while young Michael Schumacher was taking his second championship – four poles, nine wins, and Benetton (Brawn and Byrne prominent) were taking the Constructors' title – Ferrari (Alesi and Berger) had one pole and one win. Jean Todt reached for his telephone. . . .

The man Todt hired brought with him a whole array of strengths which he had finessed into a whole. He would become the highest-paid driver the world had ever seen and, however hard it would be to believe, was good value for money. Todt offered Schumacher more than $20 million per annum and Schumacher said yes.

Gary Anderson, who still speaks about Schumacher's début with Jordan in terms of reverence, has watched his subsequent career with close interest. He sets out glimpses of what Ferrari would be getting for the money.

'One year Michael had pole but the Ferrari wasn't quick enough on the straights for the race, so he said to take wing off.[1] The second section of the circuit was all about driving, not speed, and without the wing he'd lose the downforce but he said "that's my problem. I'll handle that bit – what I can't do anything about is the straight line speed."

'In 1995, Eddie Irvine said at Silverstone before he went to Ferrari "give me the same car as Michael Schumacher and I can beat him." I said "Eddie, Eddie, no way as long as you've got a hole in your behind, but I really hope you get the opportunity to find out." I worked with Eddie at Jaguar when he left Ferrari and his comment was "Michael is the best of all, full stop. Nobody's in the same league." In all four years of Eddie at Ferrari his average was eight-tenths slower in the race and nine-tenths slower in qualifying. When the car was bad the gap was much bigger but as the car got good it was closer. Michael was able to drive the bad car better. The guys who're all right in a good car can do a good job, but they don't "make" the car – Michael makes the car.'

Schumacher was Todt's great coup. Schumacher was far more than a leading driver, Schumacher was a team builder. 'At the time I came to Ferrari,' he would say, 'it was clear that it was not only a driver that was missing, it was the technical people missing.'

Martinelli, of course, was already in place. 'I was there when Michael arrived. I didn't know him personally before that – I made his acquaintance when he joined Ferrari. I had an image of him from his career up to then, very fast. My first impression? That he was kind, polite and strong-minded. He had a strong attitude to support anyone on the team towards the goal: try to improve, try to make the best car, try to win.'

During 1996, as Schumacher settled in and – almost by willpower – made the Ferrari win three times, Brawn's phone rang. . . .

Brawn was coy (to me) about how much influence

The world likes to gaze at Schumacher . . . Jerez, 1997 (top), explaining the crash with Villeneuve? Rush hour, Buenos Aires, 1998 (below).

Schumacher had wielded to get him to Maranello, contenting himself with the most diplomatic explanation that they seemed to have worked well together at Benetton.

CURRICULUM VITAE: Ross Brawn, born 23 November 1954, Manchester. Engineering apprentice at the Atomic Energy Research Establishment, Harwell, where he worked for five years. Joined Williams R & D in 1976, working on the installation of a wind tunnel. Joined Arrows as Chief Designer, Arrows were fourth in the Constructors' title in 1988. He joined Tom Walkinshaw and worked on sports cars (they won the 1991 World Championship). As joint team principal at Benetton with Flavio Briatore, Walkinshaw brought Brawn there. Seeing that Schumacher hadn't actually signed with Jordan, he brought him there too, at the end of 1991. The partnership went as far back as that, and as deep as that.

Rory Byrne, meanwhile, had retreated to Thailand where he intended to start a scuba-diving school. He had always wanted to do that and felt he had achieved as much as he could in Formula 1. After all, Benetton – only in existence since 1986 – had defeated the major teams, Ferrari and McLaren and Williams. Byrne's decision was so final that he left virtually nobody but Brawn a contact number, and only did that so Brawn could (literally) drop in if he was ever passing that way.

... The crowd watching the drivers watching the crowd at the Hungaroring, 1998.

In January 1997 the new car was being tested at Fiorano, the Ferrari test track, and Brawn watched with mounting apprehension. During subsequent testing at Jerez, Barnard, who had designed the car, departed for good. Brawn gave Todt the number Byrne had left, and Todt reached for his telephone. It rang on an island to the south of Thailand. Byrne's landlady rushed out shouting 'call for you!' and Byrne thought it must be a family crisis. When he reached the receiver he heard the cultivated French tones of Jean Todt. ...

CURRICULUM VITAE: Rory Byrne, born 10 January 1944, Pretoria. Got a BSc in industrial chemistry at university in Johannesburg ('I had to learn engineering myself!') and designed model gliders. Worked importing, making and selling things which made cars go faster. Came

to England in 1973 with a friend in Formula Ford 1600. In 1977 he met the people running Toleman, who had designs on Formula 1, and reached it in 1981. Toleman became Benetton in 1986.

The team was in place now, specifically: di Montezemolo, President; Todt, Sporting Director; Brawn, Technical Director; Byrne, Chief Designer; Martinelli, Engine Director; Gilles Simon, Engine Designer; Stepney, Team Co-ordinator who in 2001 would become Manager.

Any team, particularly if it is multi-national and spends the whole of its existence in fierce combat on a global stage – its fate always decided by fractions of a second – must be a curious creature full of exaggerated strengths and sometimes not very well concealed weaknesses. Ferrari had long been crippled by internal tensions and a sort of divine Italian madness. Years before, Alain Prost had summed it up in a phrase. Whenever Ferrari win a race, he said, there is a crisis of optimism. And Scheckter, who partnered Gilles Villeneuve at Ferrari, said that when Villeneuve reached Maranello and 'came flying into the carpark at the factory he would do a 360-degree wheelspin and the mechanics would all cheer'.[2]

Now what they were getting was proven French organisational flair, Anglo-Saxon discipline and Germanic thoroughness. Neither Ferrari nor the world would be the same again.

Brawn and Byrne had worked together since 1991 and, as Byrne has recounted, when they first met they 'talked for a couple of hours, shook hands and that was it'.[3] In 1996, when they were both still with Benetton, Byrne would say: 'One of the secrets of the company's success is how well I get on with Ross. We see eye-to-eye on virtually every issue. We very seldom disagree to a point where we have to make a fundamental decision on the way we go – his or mine. Ross is a proper Technical Director, setting procedures, establishing systems, race engineering and overall engineering programmes.'[4]

The partnership simply continued at Ferrari.

Brawn's management style was, in his own description, 'walking quietly with a big stick' and setting an example. 'You can't have a tantrum. You can't lose control and expect the people who work for you not to do the same.'[5]

Stepney has a philosophy, taught to him early on in his career by a chief mechanic: *think through what you do before it happens*. He'd keep doing that and tell the mechanics around him to do it too.

Stepney was responsible for getting the equipment and parts, estimated at 55,000lbs, to each race and co-ordinating the pit stops, now arguably the crux and the crucible of the races. These pit stops involve 20 men and Stepney rotates them so that if one is injured another can take his place (although Stepney himself fell victim to a lack

Opposite:
Horsepower
whispers as Ross
Brawn outlines
masterpieces of
movement (left

and middle).
Maybe. Or they
could be just
enjoying
themselves. The
team-builder must

understand
communal morale
(opposite right).
Malaysia, 2000, and
many at
Ferrari looked as

wonderfully silly.
The team (above),
though mercifully
not all with hair-
pieces.

of co-ordination in Spain in 2000 when, holding the fuel nozzle into Schumacher's car, he was thrown to the ground and his ankle broken as, mistakenly, Schumacher was given the signal to go).

It wasn't Schumacher's fault and Stepney pays tribute to how easy Schumacher makes it for the pit crew waiting with tyres and fuel. He stops in a 'perfect position' 99% of the time, and that makes the crew confident he'll stop *exactly* where they need him to.

Todt expresses his philosophy in a French proverb: *only mediocre people fulfil their full potential, high level people can always improve.* He would say firmly (in 1991) 'I feel that we have a very good team. I am proud of the people I've gathered around me. I like the people, I trust them at all levels.' And, on how he works: 'I want to make sure that things that have to be done the same day are done. It's energy-consuming, nerve-consuming, head-consuming, whatever, but that's the way it is. I need to be a catalyst if people need to be pushed but very often they push themselves.'[6]

There were troubles ahead, like in San Marino and Canada, 1999.

Schumacher, as Brawn attests, is a team player who keeps any problems within the team and searches for solutions within the team. Schumacher, Brawn adds, is hard and if the car isn't right he lets Brawn know all about it. Brawn appreciates the strength of this approach. No doubt the whole team appreciated Schumacher's words over the radio after he'd won the 2001 championship at the Hungaroring. 'It's so lovely to work with you guys. I love you all, I love you all, thank you.'

Martinelli, reviewing how the Time Team was created and how it began to function, says 'we have made continuous progress since the arrival of Jean Todt. You can certainly say that if you consider the steps forward since 1993: only one win in '94, only one win in '95, three wins in '96 etc etc so we have been improving year by year.'

It seems there has been a discipline in the whole team which did not exist before.

'Honestly, I think you have to start from Mr di Montezemolo – the merit came from him and Jean Todt. They have been able to organise a strong team in every area, because it cannot be just a driver alone – even if he is the best driver in Formula 1, like Michael. He cannot win if he does not have a car at a good level, an engine at a good level and so on. So we tried to improve step by step in every area and we also passed through a difficult period [the early 1990s], and I think the strength of the team has been improved by those difficulties. When you are in trouble you have to react, you have to work hard and you create a spirit: that spirit is a positive attitude by everybody.'

But one thing that everybody says about Schumacher is that he is a team player.

'Absolutely. You get everything from him, that's absolutely true. He is very focused on priorities, which are the necessary steps on any area of the vehicle. Of course I speak mainly about the engine. Michael is able to be very clever when he is doing laps in the car: which are the points that must be addressed first? He understands time, also. Normally with an engine if you have to make a modification of a component it can require not just a few seconds or hours but sometimes weeks. Of course with our racing engineer Mr D'Agostino [Giuseppe D'Agostino, Production and Chief Track Engineer], with all the designers, also sometimes we make some meetings – we have a strong chief designer of the engine, Gilles Simon. Michael is able to motivate but also to illustrate properly to the relevant people which are the topics which must be addressed.'

Is Schumacher interested in engines?

'Of course. He's very technically curious and he understands his responsibilities and what we as engineers can do, so it's a combination. He says "OK, here is a problem, you have to focus on it, you have to react." What is the critical area? Michael is very clever. He says "OK, in corners 3, 4, 5 this area of revs must be improved" – or maybe it'll be another area. This means that sometimes we can operate in a very quick way because we have very precise indications.'

Is Schumacher hard on engines?

'He is correct – he is demanding towards the engine because he's fast! You cannot be soft while using a Formula 1

The moods of the championship, 2000 . . . The start in Australia (left above) and the McLarens have already gone out of reach. On his own at Melbourne (left below) and, as the McLarens broke down, taking the win. Mayhem in Austria (above), with cars bumping through the first corner where Schumacher, touched by Ricardo Zonta's BAR and hit by Jarno Trulli's Jordan, was halted. Nothing he could do (right) but make his way back to the pits . . .

engine! When I say correct, he is very correct in his use of the engine at the top of its potential: never too much. Sometimes when we have – rarely, we can say – a reliability issue it is only due to our failure, not to him. I can put it like this: no driver abuse of engine. As you know, the best way to achieve something in motor racing is with two pedals – one for acceleration, the other for braking. . . .'

Todt, speaking after the Hungaroring in 2001, said 'for me, Schumacher is like a son, a brother, a member of the family.' Todt had said in 1999 'Michael's a great driver, a great guy. We have a group of individuals who get on very well professionally and socially, which is very important. Michael is totally committed to the team as a driver.'[7]

Irvine, Schumacher's team-mate at Ferrari from 1996 to 1999, passed his own judgement to me[8] when he said 'with Todt and Ross I learnt how a Formula 1 team should run. Rory delivered the car to Ross and Ross ran the show. That's pretty much the way it works.' Todt, of course, was unobtrusive in the sense that he drew the whole effort together; Brawn could not help but be obtrusive because he was making the tactical decisions which, with Schumacher implementing them, fascinated the global audience.

. . . Hockenheim was just as bad after Schumacher and Giancarlo Fisichella (Benetton) crashed into the first corner.

Scheckter insists that 'Schumacher's contribution has been very important to Ferrari. I have always said that he pulled the team together and many great drivers do that.'

Jackie Stewart feels that it was 'Schumacher's ability to bring that team together' which was decisive, and adds that 'at the end of the day he is the captain of the ship. No matter what di Montezemolo does, no matter how good Jean Todt is, no matter how brilliant Ross Brawn, no matter how clever Rory Byrne is, the one thing that has brought this to pass is that they all want to work for Schumacher and they all know that, given what they can provide, he will deliver. That's why they don't want to leave. If you were to go and say to Ross Brawn right now "come and work for me" he'd say "why should I work for you when I'm working for Michael Schumacher? Who's going to bring me that level of success?"

'What Schumacher has got there is a great band of real experts who'll stay – short of a few of them getting tired and leaving, like Jean Todt. Rory could too, because he's retired or tried to retire a couple of times. Ross might get tired of living in Italy. The point, however, is that for the period of time Schumacher wants to continue at that end of the business, he has enough time to win at least one more World Championship, if not two, and the great band may well stay together.'

Stewart adds this intriguing footnote. 'Schumacher has much more authority in Ferrari than Senna would ever have had. Ron Dennis totally controls McLaren, Jean Todt doesn't at Ferrari. He's an employee. Ken Tyrrell controlled his own team. Colin Chapman controlled his own team. John Cooper controlled his own team.'

The received wisdom within Formula 1 – and this goes right back to the beginning in 1950 – is that you need strong, almost dictatorial men to run it properly. They listen, they consult, they discuss, then they and they alone decide. It works for running the whole thing (Max Mosley at the FIA, Bernie Ecclestone at FOCA) and it works for running the teams (Dennis, Sir Frank Williams, Jordan, Walkinshaw, Sauber). I wonder if the real achievement at Ferrari has been to contradict this received wisdom and triumph using a corporate structure? That might just be Michael Schumacher's real triumph too: leading a team to contradict history itself.

NOTES

[1] Taking some wing off reduces the downforce and enables the car to go faster in straight lines but is an obvious disadvantage in corners where, with less downforce, you get less grip.

[2] *Gilles Villeneuve: The Life of the Legendary Racing Driver* by Gerald Donaldson (MRP, 1989).

[3] Tifosi Club website.

[4] Gran Com website.

[5] *F1 Racing* magazine.

[6] The Atlas F1 website.

[7] Ibid.

[8] *Inside the Mind of the Grand Prix Driver* (Haynes, 2001).

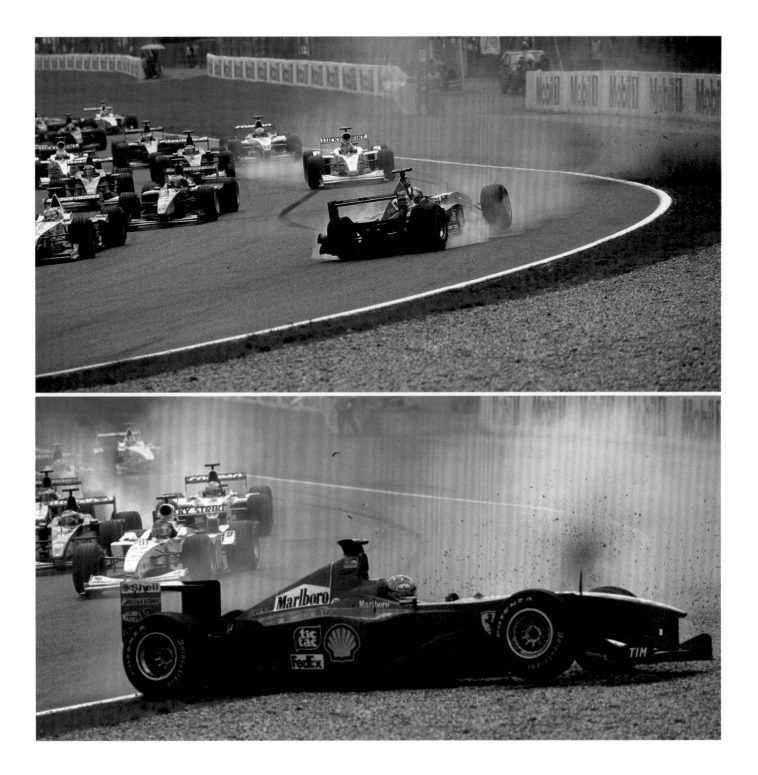

Facts of the matter

Cumulatively this is how the Ferrari Formula 1 team was reborn and then nurtured to the point where, by 2001, people spoke quite naturally of living in The Ferrari Era:

	Poles	Wins	C'tors' position	Drivers' titles	Points
1990	3	6	2	0	110
1991	0	0	3	0	55.5
Arrival of di Montezemolo					
1992	0	0	4	0	21
Arrival of Todt					
1993	0	0	4	0	28
1994	3	1	3	0	71
Arrival of Martinelli					
1995	1	1	3	0	73
Arrival of Schumacher, Brawn					
1996	4	3	2	0	70
Arrival of Byrne					
1997	3	5	2	0	102
1998	3	6	2	0	133
1999	3	6	1	0	128
2000	10	10	1	1	170
2001	11	9	1	1	179
2002	10	15	1	1	221
2003	8	8	1	1	158

Nigel Stepney ruminates on the Time Team and Schumacher. 'I know it's a team but we have all our eggs in one basket and without Michael . . . well, if you think of when Senna left McLaren, McLaren just disappeared. Same at Lotus. It's a very high risk not to have two baskets. When Michael had his accident [at Silverstone in 1999] we had Eddie Irvine and Eddie raised his level. Eddie was fighting for the championship, his level's raised – but it wasn't at the same level as Michael. When Michael came back that season he basically destroyed everybody. We learnt that if a driver has a break' – no pun intended – 'and relaxes, when he comes back he performs a lot better!

'We have a very good balance in the team generally. Everybody knows their position and nobody has any need to be negative. Everybody is doing the best they can in their area. So, OK, you always try to improve but we try to improve as a group and have confidence in the people around us to try and improve as well. We try not to change people like at Ferrari years ago when it was very unstable: you changed one person and all the people underneath changed too. It was an instability problem. Now we work in a very stable atmosphere. I was here before Todt and Ross so I survived some of the . . . [chuckle] . . . other days. Now you have a group of people but if you lose that group of people in three years I hate to think what will happen.

'The main thing is to keep up the performance. I thought after we had won the championship double once – constructors' and drivers' – what motivation have I got to win the double again? In actual fact to win it this year [2001] was better than last year because we proved it wasn't a fluke, we proved we want to go on and win more and more.'

Isn't that like certain drivers who win a World Championship and think 'I've done it' – Damon Hill, Mansell, Hunt – and other drivers like Ayrton and Michael think 'I've won one, I'm going to do this again and again'?

'That's right. You think about why you want to carry on, what motivation you've got, then you just think *it's so good to win, to be on top of everybody.*

'Michael is very professional, a very good person. Don't get me wrong: I have great respect for him too. It's not easy to work with drivers that aren't at the same level as him. That's the hardest thing. After working with Senna and Michael it's hard to accept drivers at a lower level who can't perform even when they've got the same equipment. It's not a case of these drivers trying the best they can, it's a case of whether they've got it or not. The equipment we give them is all the same, and you can't argue the toss that it isn't. That's just an excuse and at the end of the day people only accept excuses for a short time: then – *now* – you have to deliver.'

Just as Schumacher delivers and delivers and delivers.

Husband and wife team. He wins races, like the 2000 Italian Grand Prix, while she guards the family jewels – her watch and his! – at Jerez in 1994.

Chapter Six

A TEAR FOR THE PAST

A hot and dry afternoon at Imola in 1983: on lap 55 of the San Marino Grand Prix, Riccardo Patrese forced his Brabham past the Ferrari of Patrick Tambay and took the lead. The moment proved too intoxicating for Patrese who plunged off into a tyre wall. As he got out of the Brabham the crowd roared their approval – approval that he'd crashed, giving the lead back to the Ferrari. The fact that Patrese was Italian and Tambay was French mattered nothing to the Italian crowd. What did matter was Ferrari.

Tambay duly brought the Ferrari home to victory although it stopped on the slowing down lap and the crowd climbed over the barriers, swarmed the car and lifted him out of it. He had to be rescued by the police. Later he'd say it had been the most emotional day of his career, adding: 'You know, to win here in Ferrari number 27 . . . it's difficult for me to put it into words but I hope everyone understands that what happened today was more than just winning a race. Something incredible.'

The 27 Ferrari had been the one in which Gilles Villeneuve was killed a year before. Villeneuve was already a mythical figure within Ferrari. Tambay was godfather to Gilles' son Jacques.

Tambay's Ferrari (the 126 C2/B) was a beautiful car and, like so many in the turbo era, ferociously fast. In qualifying he'd averaged 197.288kmh (122mph) round Imola's twists and turns, and still only been third on the grid.

Michael Schumacher knew nothing about this sort of thing because the past did not interest him. Tambay remembers meeting him in Japan at the end of his first racing season – 1991 – and introducing himself. 'He didn't have a clue who I was or what I had done. He didn't know

The Pits Hairpin at Montreal with the ghostly reminders of Expo '76 behind. In 1998 Schumacher qualified on the second row.

I'd been a racing driver. I was just an old guy who was trying maybe to get an autograph from him. That's the feeling I had then.'

Stéphane Samson, a French journalist, had an idea. 'I am a friend of Tambay and he was always explaining how this particular race – Imola '83 – was for him. I felt it would be wonderful to have Patrick, so passionate about Ferrari, and Michael who didn't seem to care at all – just the opposite of Patrick, very rational – together, and to have Michael drive the car.' This was the spring of 1999, and no Ferrari had won at Imola since Tambay.

When it was arranged, the day would assume several degrees of importance, not least because of Schumacher's reaction to the car. It was one of the rare occasions when he has driven such a car and it afforded a glimpse – no more – of what he might have done if his career had been then. There is always a question of how, overall, a judgement can be made on the relative abilities of the greatest drivers. Versatility *must* be a factor.

The Ferrari turbo in 1983, with Patrick Tambay driving it.

Once upon a time the turbo car belonged to Tambay but 'we had a family feud, what you call a divorce. My wife's lawyers wanted to saw the thing in two and I didn't know if they wanted the front part or the back part! It had to go to an auction and it was bought by a friend of mine. He owns the car and he's run it at Goodwood[1] a couple of times. He very kindly loaned it to us for that one test.'

Samson emphasises that Schumacher 'doesn't have any historical background from Formula 1, he doesn't know anything about what happened in the 1970s or even in the 1980s. That was part of the contract we had with Michael's PR: *just don't ask him any questions about the history of the sport because he doesn't know and he doesn't care.* Apparently when he got to Ferrari he didn't know anything about the legend and he just wanted to drive for them.'

So, that spring day, the 126 was taken to Fiorano, Ferrari's test track, where Schumacher would be testing the current car, the F399. Tambay, stocky in middle age and with wisps of white threaded into his sideburns, stood lost in contemplation as it was unloaded from the transporter at 7.30am. Some of the mechanics who'd worked on it in '83 were there too.

'It was the exact chassis that won at Imola and a very emotional day because it was the first time that Patrick had gone back to Fiorano since his Ferrari days [Tambay left Ferrari at the end of 1983, joining Renault]. He had never been there since – and that race had been very strange for Patrick, because he is convinced he wasn't alone in the cockpit. He still feels that Gilles was with him, helping him,' Samson says.

In the background Schumacher hammered round and round in the F399 and, as Samson explains, 'between two runs he came to look at it. He waited until everyone was more or less away from the car, then he went around it and looked at it very carefully examining the details, trying to understand how it was working, what the exact suspension geometry was. He asked Patrick questions. I think that was, first, to understand how the car had been designed. He was very surprised to see where the radiators were – on the side pods – and very surprised by how big the wings were. I think that was second, because he wanted to check if it had been really well maintained.

'He was trying to draw confidence from this car, trying to see if he'd be able to push with it and have fun. He told me he was a bit scared when he had to drive a very old car because he always felt something could break on them. I think he was more concerned about any possibility of hurting himself than about damage to the car, although I imagine that in 1983 the drivers thought it was the best possible in terms of security!' (They did, but with great reservations, as we'll see in a moment.)

He asked Tambay how much horsepower the 126 had, and when Tambay said 1200 in qualifying and 900 in the races Schumacher said 'wow!' He asked if the pedals really were ahead of the front axle and Tambay nodded. He asked if there was anything to protect the driver's legs – it seemed they touched the suspension. Tambay said yes, they did touch it.

'That,' Schumacher concluded instantly, 'is fantastically dangerous.'

(Samson remembers clearly that Schumacher 'noticed the steering arms were more or less at the end of your legs. If he had to avoid something, and he hit the wall or the tyres, it

would really be a problem for his legs. He wasn't scared for himself [in the sense of driver error] because he knew exactly what he was going to do with the car but he said once again what he always says: *I think I wouldn't have been able to race in those days. It was too dangerous and I wouldn't be interested in doing a race with such a car'*.)

Tambay remembers 'he came to me and he looked at me in a strange way. I had the feeling that he didn't really believe I could have been a works Ferrari driver. Initially he looked at the car like it was just another piece of equipment. Then he looked at me and asked "you did actually drive this?" Obviously I'd put on weight since 1983. He was a little bit condescending, if I may say so.'

Anyway, Tambay said he had driven it.

Schumacher: 'I never could have done that, it's not safe. You have the shock absorbers and the springs, they are inboard and just protected by a little padding. Obviously there are some holes in the tub and the water can come in. The feet are way, way upfront.'

Tambay is sure that Schumacher felt the regulations under which the cars of 1983 were built had not produced safety, something Tambay and the drivers of that time had felt too, and they'd done a lot of lobbying to get the feet behind the front axle.

Schumacher: 'I don't think I would have driven that.'

Tambay: 'Of course you would. It would have been part of your era and you would have driven it and you would have gone flat out with it.'

Schumacher: 'No, no, I'm not so sure.'

'It was very interesting,' Samson says, 'to see how Michael – who doesn't pay attention to any statistics or any strange stories – listened to Patrick explaining to him about that race before Michael tested the car himself. He was quite interested, a bit curious in a way, and I sensed he didn't know what to think. You could see that. He was a bit moved by what Patrick was saying: explaining his race and describing it in a lot of detail. The tears were not far away because Patrick was very emotional.

'Before, Michael had just felt that it was driving in an old car with a normal gearbox. I think he saw that as a bit of a pain to have to do at the beginning, but then he heard the explanations. It meant that he looked at the car and he didn't know what to expect and he didn't have any particular feelings about it, but once he had listened to Patrick and he understood what the car really *meant*, he began to be more interested in it. He measured a bit more what the Ferrari legend was and what it means to so many people. I wouldn't say Michael was shaken but I would say moved by the story Patrick was telling and then by Patrick's behaviour.'

The 126 was parked outside Enzo Ferrari's house – Ferrari had a house at the circuit, and it had a number, 27, just above the door. The engine was fired up, the turbo howling and gurgling, and Schumacher was fascinated by that. As the howling echoed from in front of Enzo's house for the first time since 1983, the emotion deepened.

Schumacher went back to the F399 and did his next run. Samson wrote: 'As the afternoon draws on, the sun floods the track with a beautiful orange light. At last the driver's day job is done, and he pulls into the pits.'

Tambay says 'we were there at 7.30 in the morning and the test happened at 9.30 in the evening, so we stood the whole day waiting for him to do his ten laps in it. I said "I hope you can get a little bit of the magic of that race in '83." Stéphane and I felt that a lot of things happened when he came close to the car. The wind started blowing, leaves were turning – strange things. Stéphane noticed this and we looked at one another and we said they *were* strange things.'

The mood of Suzuka, 2000 . . . Late evening and still the crowd is there, surrounding him.

Samson wrote: 'The 126 is pushed out and, spontaneously, the old mechanics burst into applause. They know they're about to witness something special. By contrast Schumacher seems almost shy, confused. For some of these guys this chassis is real life, real memories: for him it's history. He walks slowly over, then climbs aboard. He struggles to get his legs into the aluminium cockpit, because the steering column barks against his shins and calls for some contortion. Finally, he's sitting. He adjusts his rear-view mirrors – as if automatically – and then lightly lays his hands on the steering wheel. He slowly rocks it from lock to lock, his face an expression of delight.'

Tambay, stooping towards him, gives advice and points out that the turbo doesn't like to go below 5000 revs.

Samson remembers: 'I think the last time Michael drove a single-seater with a normal [manual] gearbox was maybe the Jordan or Benetton in 1991 – and the Ferrari gearbox from '83 couldn't be compared to the Benetton gearbox from 1991! Even when he put it into first gear to move away from the pits it was smooth, the revs held perfectly. He didn't stall, he didn't get away like a maniac with smoking rubber and wheels spinning. All the mechanics were crying. It was so emotional for them. Maybe Michael understood, looking into the eyes of those guys, maybe he understood what this symbolic thing of having him drive a number 27 for the first time at Fiorano meant.'

(An aside from Tambay: 'You have to have respect for every era, every car, every mechanic, every driver because it's part of their own histories and history itself. It was very intense memories that came up to the surface again.')

'Out he went, never a single problem to pass up to second gear, third, fourth. It was always waang, waang, waang – very smooth, very quick – and Patrick was impressed. He was very kind with the car. He pushed only after two or three laps when the engine was hot and everything was working very well. He'd spent those two or three laps judging the car and playing with it, warming the tyres. He made it go fast on the straights. I think he wanted to check what the acceleration was with such a turbo charged thing. He never really pushed in the corners, basically I think because he didn't really know where the car was coming from and there was a still a feeling of *un*safety. One wheel had too much grease on it and it began to smoke and he thought the car was on fire. He did five to eight quick laps but he was not completely confident.

'When he came in and jumped from the car he said that the gearbox was awful – although he hadn't made one mistake with it – and Patrick said it was strange to hear him say that because he thought it was a beautiful gearbox, the best gearbox he'd ever had!'

Tambay says 'yes, the gearbox was as nice as bread and butter! It was a pure marvel, a marvellous piece of equipment.'

Schumacher would say: 'Technically, to drive this car means resorting to systems which are no longer current. You have to brake with the right foot, use the clutch and the conventional gearbox which only has five gears.' He'd had an impression of 'fiddling' with the gear lever the whole time. 'I never knew if it had engaged or not.'

Tambay says that, to Schumacher, 'everything must have felt hopeless, the brakes, the engine because it's a turbo – with the big turbo lag and then bang – but, then, it was the best thing available.'

Samson remains convinced that Schumacher learnt more than how to handle another old car. 'Maybe it was one of those days when you make a step towards understanding.'

Tambay had ambivalent feelings about that, although he does say: 'No team is ordinary but Ferrari obviously is something different. Schumacher said that day that he would probably start collecting his own racing cars. He didn't know if he was going to drive them because he didn't know whether in a few years he would be interested in doing that. He said he didn't know if he would be interested in having his son drive or race.

'My son is now racing and I never thought that this would happen. You mature, you grow older and wiser but when you are a racing driver you can't afford to have those thoughts and those feelings. You must be a hard, tough, racing bastard if you want to be successful the way he is!'

Samson concludes: 'I would say if he had been racing in the 1980s he would have been able to handle that car, just looking at how he used the gearbox and car. You could see that the approach he had was very professional – looking at it first, trying to understand it first and then doing the two or three laps warming everything, checking the brakes, the steering. And the way he used the gearbox: Patrick couldn't believe how smooth but efficient Michael was with that gearbox, especially as he had never driven such a thing before.'

Before we leave this, which will have relevance in Chapters Nine and Ten, here is Martin Brundle driving the 1955 Mercedes Grand Prix car. Brundle partnered Schumacher at Benetton in 1992 and of all his team-mates ran him closest. Schumacher finished on 53 points, Brundle 38. Brundle drove the Mercedes at Spa in 1998.[2]

'It's the first time I've even sat in something like this and I really didn't know what to expect. You know the driving position is going to be odd because there is a huge gearbox bellhousing between your knees so the distance between the brake pedal and the clutch must be about two feet. It's a bit like the *Doctor Who* phone box, bigger on the inside than it looks from the outside. The bonnet seems very long. You feel, too, as if you are sitting on the car rather than in it and the mirrors are like on a motorcycle: all you can see is your own shoulders. Clearly they didn't pay much attention to what was going on behind them and later on I began to understand why. You had to concentrate so bloody hard on what was going on in front of you. Physically I found the car easy to drive but mentally it was incredibly hard.

'Changing gear: these days it's a matter of 20 milli-seconds, a flick of your index finger, but on this car it's a very conscious thing. You blip, you place the lever, you push it all very deliberately. I really had to concentrate. It's quite easy, for example, to go from fifth to second which fortunately I didn't do because I imagine that would have given the engine a bit of a hurry-up.

'As far as handling was concerned, the car turned in quite nicely and the basic balance was good although there were some curious loads coming through the steering wheel. In medium speed corners like *Les Combes* you could place the car more or less where you wanted it. What about the brakes? Well, because I brake quite early for *Les Combes* anyway, at first I didn't grasp that it doesn't slow down very well, although funnily enough it seems to depend on which corner you are in and how fast you are going. Coming in to the Bus Stop, for example, it didn't seem to want to slow at all.

'I was supposed to be keeping pace with the Safety Car, and that was a special 5.5 litre Merc CLK with Jochen Mass[3] driving it: a quick car, a very quick car. And Jochen was pushing very hard, apparently, but he couldn't keep up with me. To be honest I didn't think I was going that fast but then I began to realise this car must be quite slippery through the air. I was doing 150mph through the kinks before *Blanchimont*.[4] It was at this point that I began to think about the absence of seat belts, rollover bars and the like. I began to look around and think *if you were going to hit something, what would you do?* In a modern car if you're going to crash you make sure you do certain things beforehand but with this one I really had no idea what I'd do.

'I didn't slow down because I was enjoying it so much but I did begin to feel nervous in the high-speed corners

The moods of Suzuka 2000 . . . The pits were sombre at times. . . . Practise makes perfect for the team too . . . Corinna and Schumacher's manager Willy Weber find a moment of solitude at the back of the Ferrari pit . . . The tacticians, getting it right.

because occasionally the car seemed to have a mind of its own. It was rather like flying a helicopter – that sense that if you ever let anything develop you'll have a hell of a job getting it back again. In the back of a modern Formula 1 driver's mind is the acceptance that he might get hurt doing this but it never enters your mind that you might get killed. Back then, that thought must have been right at the front of your mind and very much part of your decision-making process.

'I didn't know what to expect from this car. In terms of power perhaps it wasn't as fast as I anticipated but I had to keep reminding myself it was 44 years old and only two and a half litres. In every other way, though, I came out of it with even higher respect for the drivers of those days. I've been round the old Spa where they raced it and it is unbelievable to think they took Formula 1 cars round there. When you try and put that together with what you felt in the car . . . Jesus Christ.'

Degrees of importance: whatever Schumacher felt

about the turbo car, and Brundle felt about the 1955 Mercedes, they adapted to them almost instantly and could make them go a bit. Who can say they wouldn't have been able to do that with any car ever made? Just like Fangio, Moss and Clark did.

NOTES
[1] The Goodwood Festival of Speed, featuring cars of historical significance, is held in West Sussex, England, every summer.
[2] Interview by Nigel Roebuck, used with kind permission.
[3] Jochen Mass, incidentally, had been a tutor to Schumacher, Wendlinger and Frentzen when they came into sports cars with Mercedes, partnering each of them in the races. He refers to them as the kids, and thoroughly enjoyed the whole thing.
[4] In the car's sister, Juan-Manuel Fangio did the fastest lap of the 1955 Belgian Grand Prix on the old, full Spa – a road circuit with virtually no protection – averaging 195kmh/121mph, and won the race at an average speed of 191kmh/118mph. In the car itself Stirling Moss finished eight seconds behind Fangio.

Facts of the matter

On 1 May 1983, Patrick Tambay started third on the grid and covered 60 laps (302 kilometres) in 1h 37m 52.460s, at an average speed of 185kmh, to win the San Marino Grand Prix. He won because, as we have seen, Patrese crashed.

On 2 May 1999, Michael Schumacher started third on the grid and covered 62 laps (305 kilometres) in 1h 33m 44.792s, at an average speed of 195kmh, to win the San Marino Grand Prix. He won because Häkkinen, leading comfortably, crashed on lap 18.

This, of course, was just a few days after Schumacher drove the 126 and Samson says that 'the very good thing is that just after having driven it Michael won at Imola, the first for Ferrari there for 17 years – Patrick, 1983. Again that must have told Michael what it meant. I saw him after and although I can't remember exactly what he said it was something like 'maybe it's been useful'. It seemed a bit strange, knowing him, to say something like that. I don't think he'd considered this part of the magic could happen:

third on the grid just like Patrick, winning because Mika went off the track just like Patrese. . . .'

Tambay feels that the way it worked out was another of those strange things.

Final thoughts. The first from Tambay: 'I must say that today the car is in better shape than it was then. It was rebuilt before it was sold and it is maintained and run by the mechanics who were my mechanics then.'

The second from Samson. 'Patrick's birthday was near the time Schumacher drove the 126 and I asked Ferrari to give me one of the brake discs that Michael used to win at Imola. Michael signed this and I gave it to him and he was crying once again.'

And a Fact of Life to finish. 'We tried with *F1 Racing* magazine to have Michael drive Ferraris from the '50s, '60s, '70s and '80s,' Samson says. 'He was OK for that. "I would be delighted to do it, no problem." It didn't happen because of sponsors.'

*The moods of
Suzuka . . .
Above, body*

*shells waiting.
Below, bodies
celebrating.*

Chapter Seven

POLE TO POLE

In April 2001 Schumacher was asked[1] if his 'success had been devalued' because he had won his World Championships partnered by Jos Verstappen, JJ Lehto, Johnny Herbert and Rubens Barrichello. The implication – and meaning no disrespect to these good men – was that if Schumacher had been partnered by a genuine number one driver (as Prost had been, for example, by Lauda, then Senna) everything might have been different.

Schumacher replied: 'People always try to put it in a way that I make my team-mates slower than where they are in reality, but I think that is a load of rubbish. Why would a team be interested in slowing down another driver for his team-mate? There is no point in that.'

Indeed there isn't (and we are not talking about Austria 2002 here: that's another matter altogether). Before the start of the 2003 season, Barrichello said he felt he had improved *because* of Schumacher, this same Barrichello who, at Silverstone in 2000, became the first of Schumacher's partners to take pole. I repeat: none of the others had done it, even once. Barrichello did it again, three more times in 2002 and three times times in 2003.

Schumacher was in a stronger position than any contractual arrangements stipulated. He did deliver. Others – di Montezemolo, Todt, Brawn, Byrne, Martinelli, Stepney – were arranging the methods and the machinery of this delivery and doing so in the most effective way.

Without Schumacher, however, everything changed. Irvine couldn't deliver when Schumacher hurt himself in 1999 and,

A ritual of celebrating Schumacher's 2001 championship was enacted at Monza, however much the mood was wrong for that after the terrorist outrages of 11 September.

Until Barrichello arrived, Martin Brundle was the team-mate to stay closest to Schumacher on the track. This is Monaco 1992 (above). Schumacher talks to Symonds and Ross Brawn, on the extreme left, listens. (Right) The mutual respect between Schumacher and Brundle has lasted to this day. (Opposite) Senna wins Brazil in 1993, Schumacher is a pensive third. Both men make themselves big. Senna's total of 65 pole positions seemed to be safe for generations but Schumacher could get past it.

than the number of times team-mate Piquet had raced there. Here are their respective positions each session:

	1st practice	1st qual	2nd practice	2nd qual
Schumacher	11	5	5	5
Piquet	9	8	4	4

In that second qualifying, on a warm and overcast afternoon, Schumacher set his best time (1m 15.508) on the second of his two runs and so did Piquet (1m 15.291). From the Friday morning practice, Schumacher went progressively quicker as he became familiar with the track (1m 17.59/1m 15.44 on this Friday) but missed a gear on his fast lap in second qualifying. Schumacher would not be outqualified by a team-mate again for four years. It finished Piquet fifth (1:15.29) and Schumacher sixth (1:15.50). Pole: Senna, McLaren (1:14.04s).

Belgium (Spa), 1995. On the Friday all seemed well, Schumacher second to Berger's Ferrari (2:14.96 against 2:14.74). In the Saturday morning untimed session, however, he crashed and the car needed repairs before second qualifying. He managed ninth quickest on his first run (it had been raining), Herbert fourth. Positions shifted as the weather shifted and Schumacher made another run, this one late. Twice the gearbox electronics changed down from sixth to fifth, ramming the Renault engine up to more than 19,000 rpm, which it couldn't take. He qualified sixteenth (1:59.07), Herbert fourth (1:56.08). Pole: Berger, Ferrari (1:54.39).

Australia (Melbourne), 1996. Only one qualifying session from now on, incidentally. Schumacher's first race for Ferrari, and Eddie Irvine's too. On the Friday Schumacher qualified fourth and Irvine seventh: Irvine had had oversteer and understeer the day before (Melbourne was a new circuit, the Thursday an introduction to it) and this still didn't feel right on the Friday. It did on the Saturday and Irvine thrust in 1:32.88. Schumacher was in the spare car because the gearbox had cracked in the morning and now he had a problem with the rear wing. He sensed he could not depose the Williamses of Villeneuve and Hill on the front row but thought he might get past Irvine's 1:32.88. He did a 1:33.12s,

across four seasons, Barrichello won seven races. Direct comparison: in that time Schumacher won 35. Everybody knows the truth: a team gravitates to its own power source and revolves around that.

Everybody knows, too, that the only proper comparison for a driver is with his team-mate because (in theory, and mostly in practice) they have the same cars. Across Schumacher's thirteen Grand Prix seasons he has had nine partners and, of the 194 qualifying sessions, they managed to outqualify him only 19 times. We saw in Chapter 2 how disappointed he was not to outqualify Piquet when he made his debut at Spa in 1991. The race after that, Monza, he joined Benetton and did partner Piquet. He outqualified him with 1:22.471 against Piquet's 1:22.726.

Here are the 19 times Schumacher was outqualified. I give the pole time purely for context.

Australia (Adelaide), 1991. He had not, of course, driven Adelaide before: this was only his sixth Grand Prix, one less

Brothers in arms.
Schumacher with
Riccardo Patrese
(extreme left) who
he outqualified 16
times out of 16. He
outqualified Jos
Verstappen (left,
above) eight times
out of eight. (Left)
the shifting
currrents of a
qualifying session,
to three decimal
places. The 1997
Luxembourg Grand
Prix (above) when
he and Ralf kept
the crash at the
start in the family.
Schumacher with
Eddie Irvine
(right) who he
outqualified 55–4.

which was 0.24 of a second too slow. Irvine qualified third, Schumacher fourth. Pole: Villeneuve, Williams (1:32.37).

Austria (A1-ring), 1997. Irvine finished ahead of Schumacher although the difference was just about as close to nothing as you can reasonably get. The cars understeered, a major disadvantage at such a track. Ferrari put Irvine on soft tyres in a supreme effort to conjure a fast lap for him while Schumacher stayed on the hard Goodyear compound. He might have beaten Irvine even then but began to run out of fuel on what was potentially his hottest lap. That caused a small misfire. Irvine was eighth (1:11.051), Schumacher ninth (1:11.056). Pole: Villeneuve, Williams (1:10.30).

Germany (Hockenheim), 1998. Schumacher was decisively outqualified by Irvine this time, Irvine on the third row, Schumacher on the fifth – 'it is definitely the wrong time and the wrong place to have my worst qualifying of the season,' Schumacher said. He managed fifth after two runs but fell back as others improved. Irvine described the day as 'difficult' and a 'struggle'. Irvine qualified sixth (1:43.27), Schumacher ninth (1:43.45). Pole: Häkkinen, McLaren (1:41.83).

Spain (Barcelona), 1999. Irvine qualified on the front row, Schumacher on the second. This seemed mysterious, and Schumacher compounded that when he said that 'for reasons we must now investigate' it hadn't been as good in the afternoon as it had in the morning. This proved to be a small engine problem. Irvine finished second (1:22.21), Schumacher fourth (1:22.27). Pole: Häkkinen, McLaren (1:22.08).

Britain (Silverstone), 2000. New team-mate Barrichello took pole on a day of uncertain weather and made an early run 'because I thought it might rain later'. Schumacher changed the car's set-up for his last run. 'It did not pay off. On top of all that I made a couple of small mistakes which cost me precious time.' Pole: Barrichello (1:25.70), Schumacher fifth (1:26.16).

Austria (A1-ring), 2000. Barrichello outqualified Schumacher without extenuating circumstances.

Schumacher put it bluntly: 'On my last run I had nothing to lose: I was fourth and I gave it my all. I went over my limit at Turn 4 and lost control of the car. I am quite a way off pole time, which worries me a little. Unlike our rivals, I have been unable to find the right balance between the slow and quick corners and that is very important on this track.' Barrichello insisted firmly that 'people have been saying the gap is getting bigger between Michael and me, but that's just not right.' Barrichello finished third (1:10.84), Schumacher fourth (1:11.04). Pole: Häkkinen (1:10.41).

Italy (Monza), 2001. Many thoughts were elsewhere because the meeting at Monza began three days after the 11 September terrorist attack on the United States. Schumacher, largely silent, reflected how sombre the whole mood was and admitted that he found concentration difficult. He pushed hard enough in qualifying but his runs did not look neat or controlled. Barrichello, meanwhile, found the right set-up. Barrichello finished second (1:22.52), Schumacher third (1:22.62). Pole: Montoya, Williams (1:22.21).

Australia (Melbourne), 2002. A dry-wet session. 'Did I expect to be on pole?' Barrichello would muse. 'I feel that in life things happen for a reason. I had a strong winter testing, I feel very relaxed and I have changed my approach to my job.' He didn't elaborate. He made early runs because the forecast was for rain. 'I had traffic on my first, but the second was quick.' Schumacher said that 'the lap that counted for my grid position could have been better – because I went off onto the grass.' Barrichello pole (1m 25.843s), Schumacher alongside (1m 25.848). That's five-thousands of one second.

Austria (A1-ring), 2002. Barrichello took pole and explained: 'At Imola and in Barcelona it was close between us and Michael beat me. This time, I said to myself "not today" and tried even harder.' Mysteriously, Schumacher's racecar was slower in the qualifying session than it had been in the morning, so for his final run he switched to the spare. 'I also had problems with traffic on two of my runs.' Barrichello did

1m 08.08s, Ralf Schumacher 1m 08.36s, Schumacher (1m 08.70s) third, which he described as 'reasonable'.

Britain (Silverstone), 2002. Montoya was emerging as the man to beat in qualifying: this was his fourth consecutive pole. Schumacher, third, said 'I chose to go out earlier than usual for my first run so that we would have time to make changes to the car. The car was very good in the first sector but I was losing time in the next two. At one point, we changed the nose of the car but, to be honest, we never really got the balance right.' Montoya 1m 18.99s, Barrichello 1m 19.03s, Schumacher 1m 19.04s.

Hungary (Budapest), 2002. Barrichello took pole from Schumacher by an eye-blink. Barrichello spoke of how 'complicated' it was to set the car up here. Schumacher was equally candid. 'Rubens did a good job and I could not match it. There was no sense in trying for a final run (he did 9 laps, Barrichello 11), which is why we decided to save a set of tyres for the race. I had a wobble on my first run but it was mainly in Turn 12 that I lost time.' Barrichello 1m 13.33s, Schumacher 1m 13.39s.

Brazil (Sao Paulo), 2003. Barrichello took an emotional pole. 'I feel fantastic! Ever since I was a kid, all I wanted to do was to be here in a competitive car, waving at the crowd from pole position.' Schumacher was seventh. 'I did not manage a perfect lap,' he said. 'I made a small mistake in the first corner. Considering how close the times are' – Barrichello had done 1m 13.80s, Alonso *tenth* on 1m 14.38s – my grid position is the result of this small slip up.' Schumacher did 1m 14.13s.

Britain (Silverstone), 2003. Barrichello pole, Schumacher fifth. He said 'I made a mistake, slid and ran wide at Abbey and of course driving on grass is not very good for traction!' He described fifth as 'not the end of the world'. Barrichello described waiting for the end of the session as 'agony'. He said 'as for Michael, it was a case of mixed feelings – because of course I didn't want him to beat me but at the same time I wanted him to do well for reasons of team spirit.' Barrichello 1m 21.20s, Schumacher 1m 21.86s.

Germany (Hockenheim), 2003. Barrichello third, Schumacher sixth. Barrichello said 'I was very close to pole but I was on the limit and could not have done any better.' Schumacher said his car's handling was 'not ideal. I lost time in the second sector.' His reasoning: sixth place was particularly disappointing because the two Williams cars were on the front row but he had his nearest championship rival Kimi Räikkönen alongside him and 'we know our car performs well in terms of consistency over a long run'.

Hungary (Budapest), 2003. Barrichello fifth, Schumacher eighth. Barrichello described the session as 'rather difficult' and complained of slight understeer. Schumacher was more sombre. 'Obviously I am disappointed, because in the morning and the warm-up I seemed to be on the same pace as the others. Now we have to try and understand why our qualifying time did not match our expectations.'

USA (Indianapolis), 2003. Barrichello second, Schumacher seventh. Barrichello thought he might take pole and described his flying lap as a 'good one' even though the car felt a little loose 'all the way round'. Schumacher described it as a 'very average' session. 'I am not clear what was going on, but the car was sliding too much and I could not find any grip.' Barrichello did a 1:11.794, Schumacher 1:12.194.

Japan (Suzuka), 2003. This was the championship decider, of course, and Barrichello got out just as drizzle began. He drove what he'd describe as 'my best-ever qualifying lap at Suzuka. I drove an aggressive lap even though it was already spitting and I attacked the Esses section hard. I was all right on the fast section but I braked a bit conservatively into the chicane because by then there was a lot of water on my visor.' It gave him provisional pole, and as the drizzle hardened it became pole. Schumacher described the session as 'interesting' in his own quixotic way. 'The varying weather meant that track conditions were inconsistent.' He was fourteenth.

NOTE [1] *Autosport.*

Facts of the matter

When Barrichello took pole at Silverstone in 2000 it was the *only time* in Schumacher's career that a team-mate had ever done such a thing. The overview must be that if it was possible to force the car to take pole, Schumacher would do that – and Jos Verstappen, JJ Lehto, Johnny Herbert and Eddie Irvine, handling the same cars as he, could not. More than that, even when Schumacher had cars which couldn't get near pole he *still* forced the car to outqualify his team-mates except for these nine times.

Broadening this, I want to examine Schumacher's overall record against those pitted directly against him as his partner and, for interest, to do the same with Senna. Because they were in a sense contemporaries (between 1991 and 1994) it is possible to make a comparison in a way which is far more problematical with Fangio, Moss and Clark. I have arranged the statistics like football scores in the Qualifying column, showing which driver 'won' in terms of out-qualifying the other.

Schumacher vs his team-mates

	Races	Qual	Poles	Wins		Races	Qual	Poles	Wins
1991 (Jordan)					**1997 (Ferrari)**				
Schumacher	1	1	0	0	Schumacher	17	16	3	5
De Cesaris	1	0	0	0	Irvine	17	1	0	0
1991 (Benetton)					**1998 (Ferrari)**				
Schumacher	5	4	0	0	Schumacher	16	15	3	6
Piquet	5	1	0	0	Irvine	16	1	0	0
1992 (Benetton)					**1999 (Ferrari)**				
Schumacher	16	16	0	1	Schumacher	10	9	3	2
Brundle	16	0	0	0	Irvine	10	1	0	2
1993 (Benetton)					**2000 (Ferrari)**				
Schumacher	16	16	0	1	Schumacher	17	15	9	9
Patrese	16	0	0	0	Barrichello	17	2	1	1
1994 (Benetton)					**2001 (Ferrari)**				
Schumacher	8	8	2	5	Schumacher	17	16	11	9
Verstappen	8	0	0	0	Barrichello	17	1	0	0
Schumacher	4	4	3	3	**2002 (Ferrari)**				
Lehto	4	0	0	0	Schumacher	17	13	7	11
Schumacher	2	2	1	0	Barrichello	17	4	4	4
Herbert	2	0	0	0	**2003 (Ferrari)**				
1995 (Benetton)					Schumacher	16	10	5	6
Schumacher	16	15	4	9	Barrichello	16	6	3	2
Herbert	16	1	0	2					
1996 (Ferrari)					**TOTAL**				
Schumacher	16	15	4	3	Schumacher	194	175	55	70
Irvine	16	1	0	0	Team-mates	194	19	8	11

	Races	Qual	Poles	Wins
1984 (Toleman)				
Senna	9	7	0	0
Cecotto	9	2	0	0
Senna	2	2	0	0
Johansson	2	0	0	0
1985 (Lotus)				
Senna	16	13	7	2
De Angelis	16	3	1	1
1986 (Lotus)				
Senna	16	16	8	2
Dumfries	15[1]	0	0	0
1987 (Lotus)				
Senna	16	16	1	2
Nakajima	16	0	0	0
1988 (McLaren)				
Senna	16	14	13	8
Prost	16	2	2	7
1989 (McLaren)				
Senna	16	14	13	6
Prost	16	2	2	4

[1] Dumfries did not qualify for Monaco

	Races	Qual	Poles	Wins
1990 (McLaren)				
Senna	16	12	10	6
Berger	16	4	2	0
1991 (McLaren)				
Senna	16	13	8	7
Berger	16	3	2	1
1992 (McLaren)				
Senna	16	15	1	3
Berger	16	1	0	2
1993 (McLaren)				
Senna	13	13	0	3
Andretti	13	0	0	0
Senna	3	2	1	2
Hakkinen	3	1	0	0
1994 (Williams)				
Senna	3	3	3	0
Hill	3	0	0	0
TOTAL				
Senna	161	143	65	41
Team-mates	161	18	9	15

	Races	Qual	Poles	Wins		Races	Qual	Poles	Wins
Schumacher	194	175	55	70	Senna	161	143	65	41
Team-mates	194	19	8	11	Team-mates	161	18	9	15

That of all Schumacher's team-mates only one – Barrichello – took pole positions stands completely apart from Senna, and this may reflect that Senna had stronger team-mates, particularly Prost and Berger. Prost, however, accepted that in terms of absolute speed he could not match Senna and concentrated on racecraft, winning seven races in 1988 and four in 1989. (Interestingly, this was the same situation in 1984–85 when Lauda partnered Prost at McLaren. Lauda would remember 'I felt every bit as strong as Prost in the race proper, where I knew he didn't have the edge. The only thing was, I had to pay the penalty for poor qualifying times. To make up those places on the grid between Prost and myself, I had to take some additional risks in the race.' *To Hell and Back*, Verlag Orac, Vienna, *1985*). The point is that if Grand Prix racing was only about speed, every cowboy you meet at the traffic lights in a souped up Ford Escort would be World Champion, but they aren't.

Lauda was. Prost was. Schumacher is.

Chapter Eight

GREATEST OVERTAKING MOVE

Schumacher would say that beating Fangio's five World Championships 'is not really a target, and I don't think it would be a fair comparison anyway. What Fangio did in Formula 1 in his era was astounding. With cars going so fast and with so little safety, it appears to me exceptional, unbelievable. Without doubt I wouldn't have been able to do it. What we modern drivers do is pretty small in comparison. I've driven a fair few cars from the old days, and it is unbelievable the speeds they did.'

In 2000 Schumacher went past Senna's total of 41 wins but said 'the comparison is not honest. Ayrton was killed on the track and his record in Formula 1 would obviously have been completely different, today, without the accident.'

Prost took 193 races to win a record 51 victories, and Schumacher went past Prost in Belgium in 2001, his 158th race. All that, of course, means very little without a context, and the context has to be how strong the opposition was.

Prost's career ran concurrently with those of Piquet, Mansell and Senna himself and the quartet won 11 championships between them (not forgetting Keke Rosberg and Niki Lauda each winning one). Taking this as the yardstick, while Schumacher was winning his four championships Damon Hill managed one, Jacques Villeneuve one and Mika Häkkinen two.

Prost said at Hungary in 2001: 'When I retired at the end of 1993, I thought the first driver to reach my total would be Ayrton Senna. Alas he didn't have the time. Since then, the name Michael Schumacher imposed itself quite naturally. I

Laying rubber down as the parade lap begins at Silverstone in 1999.

think his way of leading races is closer to that of Ayrton than to mine. At times he has behaved on the track in a way that I didn't but it's hard to make comparisons. The eras are different and the cars are not at all the same. In the turbo era, reliability was limited and to win three races in a season was often an achievement. Since then, with normally-aspirated engines, Formula 1 offers clearly superior reliability. In any case, Michael is an extraordinary chap and a formidable driver. I admire very much the way he has managed his career, and also the way he manages his own image.'

In an interview with Prost, Nigel Roebuck raised the matter of Schumacher constantly having a team-mate who had to defer to him, which Prost manifestly did not (John Watson in 1980, René Arnoux in 1981–82, Eddie Cheever in 1983, Lauda in 1984–85, Rosberg in 1986, Stefan Johansson in 1987, Senna in 1988–89, Mansell in 1990, Jean Alesi in 1991, Damon Hill in 1993).

Prost said 'if I'd had a team-mate just there to help me, I could have been World Champion two times more'. Prost stressed again the pitfalls of trying to compare Senna and Schumacher. 'I don't know how you can tell, because everything is so different now, the cars, the format of the races . . . it's impossible.'

So this chapter is not a comparison, or even an attempt at one (that will be coming later). This is simply Schumacher's progress to the record number of wins. Incidentally, Schumacher felt the best were Belgium 1992, Belgium 1995, Belgium 1996, Monza 1996, Monaco 1997, Budapest 1998, and Suzuka 2000.

That of these seven, three should be at Spa seems significant because as a circuit – and never forgetting the caprices of the weather – it is much closer to the traditional notion of racing than anywhere else. The significance of *that* is: however much Schumacher protests about the dangerous old days, the one circuit reflecting the old days, albeit distantly, is where he has been so dominant.

The 70 wins . . .

Here they are, in sequence. It starts to get serious at win number 24 when he went past thrice World Champion Nelson Piquet's total. By number 28 he had Fangio, Lauda, Clark and Stewart behind him. Three drivers remained in the great overtaking panorama: Mansell on 31, Senna on 41 and Prost on 51 . . .

BELGIUM, 1992 (Benetton)

Second row. Spa offered its usual tantalising micro-climate. Schumacher pitted for wet tyres on lap four and worked his way from ninth place to third – then he went off and came back on behind his team-mate Martin Brundle. Schumacher noticed that Brundle's tyres were worn and 'immediately called the team' so that he could come in to change his own. He did – to slicks, the first of the front runners to do that. He led, and although Mansell in the Williams was catching him the exhaust on the Williams broke. *Podium: Schumacher 1h 36m 10.72s, Mansell @ 36.59s, Patrese (Williams) @ 43.89s.*

PORTUGAL, 1993 (Benetton)

Third row. He ran fifth to the first pit stops, then second behind Prost (Williams), and he decided not to make a second stop (for tyres – there was no refuelling in 1993). Prost pitted late – lap 29 – giving the lead to Schumacher. Prost hunted and harried him but couldn't get past. *Podium: Schumacher 1h 32m 46.30s, Prost @ 0.98s, Hill (Williams) @ 8.20s.*

BRAZIL, 1994 (Benetton)

Front row. Senna had pole and made a swift start, Alesi (Ferrari) nipping past Schumacher who needed a lap to re-take him. Schumacher led after the pit stops and cruised home once Senna, pursuing hard, spun off. By the end he had lapped the whole field. *Podium: Schumacher 1h 35m 38.75s, Hill @ 1 lap, Alesi @ 1 lap.*

PACIFIC, 1994 (Benetton)

Front row. Schumacher seized the lead from Senna (pole) who collided with Nicola Larini (Ferrari) at the first corner. Schumacher gave a crushing performance after that, so crushing that he didn't even lose the lead during his two pit stops. Again he lapped the whole field – except Berger (Ferrari). *Podium: Schumacher 1h 46m 01.69s, Berger @ 1m 15.30s, Barrichello (Jordan) @ 1 lap.*

SAN MARINO, 1994 (Benetton)

Front row. Senna dead, and a chilled, joyless victory in the wake of that. *Podium: Schumacher 1h 28m 28.64s, Nicola Larini (Ferrari) @ 54.94s, Häkkinen (McLaren) @ 1m 10.67s.*

MONACO, 1994 (Benetton)

Pole. Schumacher the reluctant inheritor of Senna's mantle: he drew the circuit of Monaco to him and laid his will across it, leading every lap. He led Berger by some 4 seconds after the opening lap (which made people reach back to Jim Clark for anything approaching this), made his first pit stop on lap 24 with enough time to keep the lead and did the same again at his second stop. *Podium: Schumacher 1h 49m 55.37s, Martin Brundle (McLaren) @ 37.27s, Berger @ 1m 16.82s.*

CANADA, 1994 (Benetton)

Pole. Schumacher had Alesi alongside and Berger behind. Schumacher – slow at the start – muscled the Ferraris and pulled away. He was making one stop and wasn't sure what the Ferraris were doing (Berger was to stop twice, Alesi once). Schumacher pulled further away and, when he felt absolutely secure, eased off, looking after the brakes and tyres. *Podium: Schumacher 1h 44m 31.88s, Hill (Williams) @ 39.66s, Alesi @ 1m 13.38s.*

FRANCE, 1994 (Benetton)

8

Second row. Schumacher made a tremendous start to lead but was harried by Hill (Williams). They both pitted on lap 21, Schumacher taking on less fuel than Hill. It was the pivotal moment, Schumacher due to stop three times and now drawing decisively away from Hill in a sustained sprint. Although Hill took the lead when Schumacher stopped again, Schumacher was now on fresh tyres and as Hill pitted a second time Schumacher vanished into the distance – emerging from the third stop he had 15 seconds over Hill and it was ample. *Podium: Schumacher 1h 38m 35.70s, Hill @ 12.64s, Berger @ 52.76s.*

HUNGARY, 1994 (Benetton)

9

Pole. Hill made a better start but Schumacher drove round the outside of him into the first corner and although Hill regained the lead when Schumacher made his first pit stop, the shape of the race was established: Schumacher on a three-stop strategy again, Hill on two, so that when Hill did stop Schumacher sailed by not to be caught again. *Podium: Schumacher 1h 48m 00.18s, Hill @ 20.82s, Jos Verstappen (Benetton) @1m 10.32s.*

EUROPE, 1994 (Benetton)

10

Pole. Hill took an immediate lead – but Schumacher was on three stops again. Hill led to the first of them but, after his own, found Schumacher ahead. Hill's refuelling rig had a problem and he couldn't take on as much fuel as he needed, forcing him to make his second stop early. Schumacher was gone towards victory by then. *Podium: Schumacher 1h 40m 26.68s, Hill @24.68s, Häkkinen @ 1m 09.64s.*

BRAZIL, 1995 (Benetton)

11

Front row. Schumacher led Hill as they completed lap 1 but Hill stayed with him. Schumacher pitted first and Hill used Schumacher's own tactic – a lung-bursting sprint – to build a margin, so that he retained the lead after his own pit stop. Hill, however, spun off when the car locked. Schumacher made his second stop of three, passing the lead to Coulthard, but caught up as Coulthard made his second stop. Schumacher sprinted himself and built a margin large enough to protect his third stop. *Podium: Schumacher 1h 38m 34.15s, Coulthard (Williams) @ 8.06s, Berger (Ferrari) @ 1 lap.*

SPAIN, 1995 (Benetton)

12

Pole. Schumacher powered into the lead, from Alesi, and held him at bay comfortably enough. Then he stretched the lead at around a second a lap – and he would only stop twice. Hill, moving up to second place when Alesi's engine failed, would stop three times. Superficially it seemed Hill might challenge him but the third stop proved too much. *Podium: Schumacher 1h 34m 20.50s, Herbert (Benetton) @ 51.98s, Berger (Ferrari) @ 1m 05.23s.*

MONACO, 1995 (Benetton)

Front row. Hill had pole but Schumacher claimed after the race that Benetton knew Hill would be stopping twice. They selected a single stop for themselves. Hill led but Schumacher, even carrying a heavier fuel load, was able to stay with him. When Hill made his first stop, on lap 23 of the 78, Schumacher was gone. *Podium: Schumacher 1h 53m 11.25s, Hill @ 34.81s, Berger @ 1m 11.44s.*

FRANCE, 1995 (Benetton)

Front row. Hill led, Schumacher behind. Benetton had a fluid pit stop strategy – two or three, as the race developed – and now Schumacher harried Hill. Schumacher pitted first and, emerging, found enough time to gain the lead when Hill pitted. Schumacher retained this through the second pit stops to the end. *Podium: Schumacher 1h 38m 28.42s, Hill @ 31.30s, Coulthard @ 1m 02.82s.*

GERMANY, 1995 (Benetton)

Front row. Hill led but, moving into the second lap, inexplicably went off at the first corner, presenting Schumacher with the race. Coulthard (Williams) struggled to stay with him and eventually fell away. It was all as simple as that. *Podium: Schumacher 1h 22m 56.04s, Coulthard @ 5.98s, Berger (Ferrari) @ 1m 08.09s.*

BELGIUM, 1995 (Benetton)

Eighth row. A chaotic build-up for Benetton, beset by Schumacher going off on the Saturday morning and the car having a gearbox problem. Wet qualifying produced a surreal grid, with Hill on the fourth row. From the eighth row Schumacher constructed a magnificent race. Completing lap 1 he was thirteenth, lap 2 tenth, lap 3 eighth, laps 4 and 5 seventh, laps 6 to 10 fifth, laps 11 to 13 fourth, lap 14 third (Hill now in the lead), lap 15 second – which became the lead as Hill pitted. A bewildering race too: at one point Schumacher circled on dry tyres in the wet. (It must also be said that, at moments, Schumacher kept Hill back very robustly indeed.) A late 10-second stop 'n' go penalty for Hill, for speeding in the pit lane, finally killed the race as a contest. *Podium: Schumacher 1h 36m 47.87s, Hill @ 19.49s, Brundle (Ligier) @ 24.99s.*

EUROPE, 1995 (Benetton)

Second row. Coulthard led from Schumacher – both on wet tyres – but Alesi (Ferrari) was on slicks and moved up from sixth. That produced a rush to the pits for slicks and gave Alesi the lead. Coulthard ran second but Schumacher overtook him. Schumacher caught Alesi although, on lap 52 of the 67, he had to make a third stop. The first had been essentially a tyre change, not much fuel put in. He emerged 24 seconds behind Alesi, with 16 laps left. Hill's Williams skated off the circuit, virtually giving the World Championship to Schumacher. He reasoned that he could attack with impunity, caught Alesi and – Alesi on worn tyres after only one stop – plundered the lead at the chicane, forcing Alesi to go wide or crash. *Podium: Schumacher 1h 39m 59.04s, Alesi @ 2.68s, Coulthard @ 35.38s.*

PACIFIC, 1995 (Benetton)

Second row. Schumacher confirmed the championship with deft Benetton strategy, which again they'd left fluid. Coulthard led in mid-race, Schumacher behind him, but Schumacher reversed that when Coulthard made his second stop. You know the rest: Schumacher at full bore and building enough of a margin to stop again and still win. *Podium: Schumacher 1h 48m 49.97s, Coulthard @ 14.29s, Hill @ 48.33s.*

JAPAN, 1995 (Benetton)

Pole. After drizzle everyone was on wet weather tyres. Schumacher led from Alesi and pulled away but Alesi drew up, only to be punished with a 10-second stop 'n' go penalty for jumping the start. That was lap 5 and two laps later Alesi was in again, for slicks. Schumacher was in for slicks himself on lap 10 while Alesi scythed up to second place. They duelled until the Ferrari's driveshaft failed and Schumacher ran smoothly home. *Podium: Schumacher 1h 36m 52.93s, Häkkinen @ 18.33s, Herbert @ 1m 23.80s.*

SPAIN, 1996 (Ferrari)

Second row. Schumacher's first masterpiece of movement at Ferrari (it was his seventh race for them). In abominably wet conditions he made a faltering start, hampered by a clutch problem, and could see so little that he didn't know what position he was in or even how many cars he overtook on the first lap. It was probably three or four. He finished that lap sixth and now Irvine in the other Ferrari spun (fifth), then Hill made a mistake (fourth). He overtook Berger in the Benetton (third), on lap 9 overtook Alesi in the other Benetton (second) and three laps later sailed past Villeneuve into the lead. He was driving at a different level from all the others, his sensitivity creating certainty where ten others crashed or spun off. *Podium: Schumacher 1h 59m 49.30s, Alesi @ 45.30, Villeneuve (Williams) @ 48.38s.*

BELGIUM, 1996 (Ferrari)

Second row. Schumacher's second masterpiece of movement, pressing the art of the possible to its limit. Villeneuve was fast away but Schumacher beat Hill into *La Source*. He set off after Villeneuve but couldn't catch him. The pace car was out at lap 13 (Verstappen's Footwork had crashed) and Schumacher pitted almost immediately, Villeneuve not for another two laps because of confusion in the Williams pit. Schumacher was feeling 'a lot of play' on the steering wheel – he'd been riding the kerbs hard to stay with Villeneuve at the start – and now stayed away from the kerbs. He made a second stop. Villeneuve emerged from his second stop fractionally ahead but Schumacher powered by into *Eau Rouge*. *Podium: Schumacher 1h 28m 15.12s, Villeneuve @ 5.60s, Häkkinen @ 15.71s.*

ITALY, 1996 (Ferrari)

Second row. As the race settled, Alesi led from Schumacher. Alesi made his only pit stop on lap 31 but Schumacher stayed out another couple of laps: long enough for him to travel at a searing pace and emerge from his own stop in the lead. He made only one mistake – a lapse of concentration, he'd admit – when he clipped the tyre markers at the chicane [the tyres were to stop the drivers riding the full width of the kerbing]. Schumacher clipped them so hard that the steering wheel was plucked from his hands. He re-gathered the Ferrari smoothly enough. *Podium: Schumacher 1h 17m 43.63s, Alesi @ 18.26s, Häkkinen @ 1m 06.63s.*

MONACO, 1997 (Ferrari)

Front row. Drizzle before the race, rain on the parade lap – and Schumacher had risked choosing the 'intermediate' Ferrari rather than the one set up for the dry. The Williamses were on slicks and so was Häkkinen. Schumacher simply drove away from them, with Giancarlo Fisichella (Jordan) in second place but falling away every lap. Barrichello (Stewart) took over second place and circled in the distance while, on lap 53, Schumacher went up the escape road at *Ste Devote* but very deliberately rotated the Ferrari and returned, effortlessly. *Podium: Schumacher 2h 00m 05.65s, Barrichello @ 53.30s, Irvine @ 1m 22.10s.*

CANADA, 1997 (Ferrari)

Pole. Schumacher led but at his first pit stop gave that to Coulthard (McLaren) who, it seemed, would win; but the pace car was out after Olivier Panis (Prost) crashed and Coulthard, making a final stop, found that the McLaren stalled. He came back out but the race finished under the pace car so he could do nothing but follow it. *Podium: Schumacher 1h 17m 40.64s, Alesi @ 2.56s, Fisichella @ 3.21s.*

FRANCE, 1997 (Ferrari)

Pole. Schumacher led from Frentzen (Williams) and it became a procession until, on lap 60 of the 72, heavy rain fell. On lap 63 Schumacher, holding an enormous lead, went off but recovered and continued *on slick tyres* to the end. *Podium: Schumacher 1h 38m 50.49s, Frentzen @ 23.53s, Irvine @ 1m 14.80s.*

BELGIUM, 1997 (Ferrari)

Second row. The race started under the pace car because the track was wet. As at Monaco, Schumacher selected the 'intermediate' Ferrari. The pace car pulled off and, completing lap 4, Villeneuve led from Alesi and Schumacher. At *La Source* he went inside Alesi and at Rivage, the right-loop out in the country, he surged past Villeneuve. The race was decided. *Podium: Schumacher 1h 33m 46.71s, Fisichella @ 26.75s, Frentzen @ 32.14s.*

JAPAN, 1997 (Ferrari)

Front row. Ferrari hatched a plan because Villeneuve had been banned from the race (failing to slow under a warning flag in Saturday free practice) but reinstated under appeal. Villeneuve, anticipating that he'd lose the appeal and forfeit any points he got in the race, aimed to hold Schumacher back: they were locked into a struggle for the World Championship. Villeneuve led, Schumacher let Irvine by – but made sure Häkkinen couldn't follow – and Irvine took Villeneuve. A complex race, Schumacher getting ahead of Villeneuve at the first pit stops and Irvine backed off to let Schumacher by, then making sure Villeneuve couldn't follow. *Podium: Schumacher 1h 29m 48.44s, Frentzen @ 1.37s, Irvine @ 26.38s.*

ARGENTINA, 1998 (Ferrari)

Front row. Coulthard, pole, led but Schumacher elbowed through on lap 5: the cars touched. Schumacher was able to continue at full speed and the race turned on whether he could gain enough time to stop twice – Häkkinen was only stopping once. Schumacher could, and did. *Podium: Schumacher 1h 48m 36.17s, Häkkinen @ 22.89s, Irvine @ 57.74s.*

CANADA, 1998 (Ferrari)

Second row. Coulthard led from Schumacher to lap 19, when the McLaren's throttle linkage failed. Schumacher pitted and, emerging, seemed not to notice Frentzen coming up at him – Frentzen went off. Schumacher had to serve a 10-second stop 'n' go penalty for that. Fisichella led but both he and Schumacher had to make pit stops. When Fisichella stopped Schumacher stayed out another five laps, plundering fastest laps to protect his own stops. *Podium: Schumacher 1h 40m 57.35s, Fisichella @ 16.66s, Irvine @ 1m 00.05s.*

FRANCE, 1998 (Ferrari)

Front row. Schumacher made an extraordinary start, consolidated that and ran to the end for, perhaps, the most straightforward victory of his career so far. *Podium: Schumacher 1h 34m 45.02s, Irvine @ 19.57s, Häkkinen @ 19.74s.*

BRITAIN, 1998 (Ferrari)

Front row. The bizarre, surreal race: on lap 43 Schumacher, running second, lapped the Benetton of Alexander Wurz under a yellow flag – the track was awash. The stewards waited for 28 minutes – three minutes longer than the time limit for notification – before telling Ferrari that Schumacher would be given a 10-second penalty. There was also confusion over the application of the rules. Häkkinen slithered off and, as a precaution, Ferrari brought Schumacher in for the penalty on the final lap. It meant Schumacher crossed the line on the pit lane and won the race stationary. In fact the 10-second penalty was rescinded. *Podium: Schumacher 1h 47m 12.45s, Häkkinen @ 12.46s, Irvine @ 19.19s.*

HUNGARY, 1998 (Ferrari)

Second row. The race was decided by something approaching sleight of hand. Häkkinen led from Coulthard, Schumacher third. After the first pit stops Schumacher ran fourth behind Villeneuve and the team decided to move to a three-stop strategy. Villeneuve pitted, Schumacher sprinted and made his second stop – only 6.8 seconds. That and the sprint enabled him to lead after the McLarens had pitted. Ross Brawn told him he had to build a lead of 25 seconds in 19 laps to protect his third stop. Schumacher sprinted again and led by 29 seconds when he did stop. It was enough. *Podium: Schumacher 1h 45m 25.55s, Coulthard @ 9.43s, Villeneuve @ 44.44s.*

ITALY, 1998 (Ferrari)

Pole. Schumacher made a poor start and reached the first chicane fifth. He took Villeneuve to be fourth and, when Irvine had let him through, tracked the McLarens of Häkkinen and Coulthard but couldn't immediately get near them. When Coulthard's engine failed on lap 17, Schumacher took Häkkinen, who had handling problems anyway. *Podium: Schumacher 1h 17m 09.67s, Irvine at 37.97s, Ralf Schumacher (Jordan) @ 41.15s.*

SAN MARINO, 1999 (Ferrari)

Second row. Häkkinen led from Coulthard, Schumacher third, but at the end of lap 17 Häkkinen rode a kerb and the McLaren snapped into the wall. Schumacher realised he couldn't catch Coulthard and Ferrari moved to a two-stop strategy (Coulthard was on one). It meant Schumacher sprinted, closed up, pitted and had three clear laps to gain time before Coulthard pitted. He did, and held a five-second lead after his second stop. *Podium: Schumacher 1h 33m 44.79s, Coulthard @ 4.26s, Barrichello @ 1 lap.*

MONACO, 1999 (Ferrari)

Front row. Schumacher made a tremendous start, beating Häkkinen, pole, to *Ste Devote* and building a lead from there. He had soon settled to a pace Häkkinen couldn't stay with and made his single pit stop in great safety, emerging still in the lead. ***Podium: Schumacher 1h 49m 31.81s, Irvine at 30.47s, Häkkinen @ 37.48s.***

AUSTRALIA, 2000 (Ferrari)

Second row. An inherited win – or was it? The McLarens of Häkkinen and Coulthard filled the front row, Häkkinen led from Coulthard but Schumacher was able to stay with them without 'pushing'. Coulthard dropped out on lap 12 with an engine failure and Häkkinen dropped out on lap 19 with an engine failure too. Race over. ***Podium: Schumacher 1h 34m 01.98s, Barrichello (Ferrari) @ 11.41s, Ralf Schumacher (Williams) @ 20.00s.***

BRAZIL, 2000 (Ferrari)

Second row. McLaren, filling the front row again, selected a one-stop strategy, Ferrari two. That meant Schumacher had to get ahead of the McLarens as soon as possible and pull away from them. Schumacher did that, beating Coulthard from the line and overtaking Häkkinen as they moved into lap 2. Schumacher made his first stop on lap 20 but emerged 6.7 seconds behind Häkkinen. The race hung in a fine balance but Häkkinen's engine failed. Yes: race over – again. ***Podium: Schumacher 1h 31m 35.27s, Fisichella (Benetton) @ 39.89s, Frentzen (Jordan) @ 42.25s.***

SAN MARINO, 2000 (Ferrari)

Front row. Häkkinen led, Schumacher after him – and Häkkinen held him to the first pit stops at virtually the mid-point of the race. However Häkkinen made his second stop early and that gave Schumacher three laps to sprint before his own. The familiar story. Schumacher sprinted hard enough to pit and keep the lead. ***Podium: Schumacher 1h 31m 39.77s, Häkkinen @ 1.16s, Coulthard @ 51.00s.***

EUROPE, 2000 (Ferrari)

Front row. Häkkinen made an astonishing start, touching the Ferrari (which irritated Schumacher) and they ran in that order, Coulthard third. Rain fell and Schumacher applied pressure, slicing past Häkkinen at the chicane and pulling away – but both needed wet tyres and pitted for them. Schumacher led and, with the weather getting worse, stroked the Ferrari to go faster and faster. He made his second stop and took on enough fuel to run to the end. Häkkinen, pitting ten laps later, hadn't created enough of a gap to do that and keep the lead. Häkkinen pressed hard but Schumacher's control was never seriously threatened. ***Podium: Schumacher 1h 42m 00.30s, Häkkinen @ 13.82s, Coulthard @ 1 lap.***

CANADA, 2000 (Ferrari)

Pole. Schumacher led from Coulthard and these two pulled away but Coulthard's engine had stalled before the parade lap and restarting it took longer than the regulations, bringing a 10-second stop 'n' go. Coulthard served that, his chances essentially destroyed. The weather broke and Schumacher tip-toed home despite, at one point, going off. *Podium: Schumacher 1h 41m 12.31s, Barrichello @ 0.17s, Fisichella (Benetton) @ 15.36s.*

ITALY, 2000 (Ferrari)

Pole. The sad win. Schumacher was leading as the race began but a crash elsewhere cost the life of a marshal. The pace car was out for ten laps and when it was gone Schumacher constructed a big lead over Häkkinen. It was enough. Afterwards Schumacher cried because he'd won at Ferrari's spiritual home of Monza – and stopped Häkkinen's charge: Häkkinen had won the last two races. *Podium: Schumacher 1h 27m 31.63s, Häkkinen @ 3.81s, Ralf Schumacher @ 52.43s.*

USA, 2000 (Ferrari)

Pole. Coulthard inadvertently jumped the start and led, Schumacher behind and calculating that Coulthard would be getting a 10-second stop 'n' go but feeling that Coulthard was holding him back so team-mate Häkkinen could attack. Schumacher took Coulthard on the inside. It rained briefly. Schumacher stayed on wet tyres until lap 16 and emerged still 11 seconds ahead of Häkkinen. Although Häkkinen cut deep into that, the McLaren's engine let go. *Podium: Schumacher 1h 36m 30.88s, Barrichello @ 12.11s, Frentzen @ 17.36s.*

JAPAN, 2000 (Ferrari)

Pole. The World Championship decider and Häkkinen led away, Schumacher behind. They circled together but Häkkinen held the lead through the first pit stops. Towards the second stops it drizzled and Häkkinen was in on lap 37 giving Schumacher two clear laps to sprint. He did and was able to stop and emerge with a four second lead. It rained and Schumacher had to treat his dry tyres cautiously. Häkkinen wouldn't surrender but Schumacher, even easing back, could not be caught. Ferrari had their first World Champion since 1979. *Podium: Schumacher 1h 29m 53.43s, Häkkinen @ 1.83s, Coulthard @ 1m 09.91s.*

MALAYSIA, 2000 (Ferrari)

Pole. Schumacher and Häkkinen rolled before the lights but Häkkinen broke the beam and Schumacher did not. Häkkinen would have a 10-second stop 'n' go. He led from Coulthard, Schumacher third. Anticipating the penalty, Häkkinen let Coulthard through. Coulthard began to construct a lead but on lap 13 went briefly off and pitted earlier than he would have done: grass in the radiator. Schumacher went through and, although Coulthard challenged him late in the race, he couldn't get past. *Podium: Schumacher 1h 35m 54.23s, Coulthard @ 0.73s, Barrichello @ 18.44s.*

AUSTRALIA, 2001 (Ferrari)

Pole. Another sad win, a marshal killed by a wheel from Villeneuve's BAR. Schumacher led from Häkkinen, the pace car came out following the Villeneuve accident and when it had gone Schumacher accelerated away from Häkkinen hard. Not that that mattered. Häkkinen's suspension failed and Schumacher moved comfortably to the victory. *Podium: Schumacher 1h 38m 26.53s, Coulthard @ 01.72s, Barrichello @ 33.49s.*

MALAYSIA, 2001 (Ferrari)

Pole. Schumacher moved cleanly away from Barrichello but on lap 3 both went off – and came back on (Schumacher 11th) – in rain which a lap later increased heavily. The rush to the pits for wets began and, settling after that, Schumacher cut through the field and led on lap 16. From there the Ferraris ran safely home. *Podium: Schumacher 1h 47m 34.80s, Barrichello @ 23.66s, Coulthard @ 28.55s.*

SPAIN, 2001 (Ferrari)

Pole. The lucky one. In fact it was so lucky that Schumacher said he didn't care to win races like this. He led from Häkkinen and held that through the first pit stops, even increasing it a little. He made his second stop on lap 43, Häkkinen seven laps later and with enough time to retain the lead. More than that, Schumacher had a severe vibration and slowed. Häkkinen moved into the final lap some 40 seconds ahead – and the clutch exploded. *Podium: Schumacher 1h 31m 03.30s, Montoya (Williams) @ 40.74s, Villeneuve @ 49.63s.*

MONACO, 2001 (Ferrari)

Front row. Coulthard, pole, had a problem getting away on the parade lap and started from the back, leaving a clear path for Schumacher into *Ste Devote* and the wide blue yonder. He went there. Häkkinen, second, retired on lap 16 with a suspension problem and Schumacher moved inevitably to victory. It was, as he said himself, straightforward. *Podium: Schumacher 1h 47m 22.56s, Barrichello @ 00.43s, Irvine @ 30.69s.*

EUROPE, 2001 (Ferrari)

Pole. Ralf Schumacher pressed his brother hard in the opening stages after a muscular start between the two but had a 10-second stop 'n' go penalty for crossing the white line coming from the pits, and the race was over. *Podium: Schumacher 1h 29m 42.72s, Montoya @ 4.22s, Coulthard @ 24.99s.*

FRANCE, 2001 (Ferrari)

Front row. Ralf, pole, led while his brother fended off Coulthard and then laid the pressure on. Ralf had a slow first pit stop, costing the lead, and his Williams was difficult to drive. Big brother pulled away and only lost the lead to Montoya during the second stops, regaining it when Montoya pitted. *Podium: Schumacher 1h 33m 35.63s, Ralf Schumacher @ 10.40s, Barrichello @ 16.38s.*

HUNGARY, 2001 (Ferrari)

Pole. A consummate drive, during which he only lost the lead during his pit stops, gave Schumacher his fourth World Championship and equalled Prost's total of wins. Schumacher had looked invincible all weekend, and was. *Podium: Schumacher 1h 41m 49.67s, Barrichello @ 3.36s, Coulthard @ 3.94s.*

BELGIUM, 2001 (Ferrari)

Second row. Montoya, pole, stalled before the parade lap and started from the back. The race was stopped after Luciano Burti (Prost) crashed heavily on lap 4 and, moving into the formation lap for the re-start, Ralf's Williams was still being worked on – he'd start from the back. Schumacher's second row position had become pole by default and he led the race throughout to – finally – overtake Prost. *Podium: Schumacher 1h 08m 05.00s, Coulthard @ 10.10s, Fisichella @ 27.74s.*

JAPAN, 2001 (Ferrari)

Pole. This was his eleventh of the season, a record for Ferrari. In the race he pulled away from the Williamses of brother Ralf and Montoya so comprehensively that after three seconds he held a lead of more than eight seconds. Apart from the two pit stops he led throughout, had sets of spare tyres in abundance and, as it would seem, spare pace if he ever needed it. He didn't. *Podium: Schumacher 1h 27m 33.29s, Montoya @ 3.15s, Coulthard @ 23.26s*

AUSTRALIA, 2002 (Ferrari)

First row, Barrichello pole. The beginning of a season of almost absolute domination. This was emphasised by the fact that Ferrari used the previous season's car. Schumacher ran fourth early on but, after some spirited duelling with Montoya, took the lead by lap 17 and didn't lose it. *Podium: Schumacher 1h 35m 33.29s, Montoya @ 18.62s, Räikkönen @ 25.06s.*

BRAZIL, 2002 (Ferrari)

55

Front row, Montoya pole. The new car appeared at last and with it Schumacher gave Montoya a visit to the chopping board, which did not please Montoya at all. He lost his front wing while Schumacher continued to a victory from his brother, who preferred to hold station rather than risk the six points. *Podium: Schumacher 1h 31m 43.66s, Ralf Schumacher @ 0.58s, Coulthard @ 59.10s.*

SAN MARINO, 2002 (Ferrari)

56

Pole, from Barrichello. Schumacher took the lead at the lights, Ralf up to second from Barrichello. Completing lap one, Schumacher led by 1.3 seconds and that was both a portent and a preview. Schumacher led every lap except during his two pit stops and only Barrichello threatened to challenge him. Even that melted away when Barrichello had a wheelnut problem. *Podium: Schumacher 1h 29m 10.78s, Barrichello @ 17.90s, Ralf Schumacher @ 19.75s.*

SPAIN, 2002 (Ferrari)

57

Pole, from Barrichello. Again Barrichello had seemed the sole challenger – in qualifying they were the only ones in the 1m 16s – but he took no part in the race, having a gear selection problem on the grid. Schumacher won the race so easily that Brawn told him he had to stay awake. He did this by setting fastest laps at will. *Podium: Schumacher 1h 30m 29.98s, Montoya @ 35.63s, Coulthard @ 42.62s.*

AUSTRIA, 2002 (Ferrari)

58

Second row, Barrichello pole. The race that descended into bitter controversy because Barrichello, having led throughout, was ordered to move aside to give the win to Schumacher who already had 44 points to Montoya's 23. On the run to the line Barrichello obeyed the team orders, which had been radioed to him, Schumacher swept by and the podium ceremony was met with hoots of derision. *Podium: Schumacher 1h 33m 51.56s, Barrichello @ 0.18s, Montoya @ 17.73s.*

CANADA, 2002 (Ferrari)

59

Front row, Montoya pole. A curiosity, this season: Schumacher did not have a smooth passage. He went for a one-stop strategy (Barrichello and Montoya on two) and although he had the lead for the final stages, he was nursing a blistered tyre – and Montoya was catching him. After 56 laps Montoya's engine failed. *Podium: 1h 33m 36.11s, Coulthard @ 1.13s, Barrichello @ 7.08s.*

BRITAIN, 2002 (Ferrari)

Second row, Montoya pole. Barrichello, on the front row, had more misfortune with gear problems before the start. That left Schumacher and Montoya: Schumacher took him on lap 16 after the first pit stops and commanded the race from there. In fact Barrichello, working his way up from the back, might actually have challenged Schumacher – but spun. *Podium: Schumacher 1h 31m 45.01s, Barrichello @ 14.57s, Montoya @ 31.66s.*

FRANCE, 2002 (Ferrari)

Front row, Montoya pole. The championship race, and it was only round eleven. Nobody else in modern history, apart from Nigel Mansell (1992), had done it this early, although the showdown was by no means straightforward. Montoya led to the first pit stops, Schumacher was given a drive-through penalty for crossing the white line on exiting the pits and ran third. He thought the championship would have to wait. Towards the end he hounded Räikkönen who slithered on oil. Game over. *Podium: Schumacher 1h 32m 09.83s, Räikkönen @ 1.10s, Coulthard @ 31.97s.*

GERMANY, 2002 (Ferrari)

Pole. By now any competitive aspect to the season had long gone and the thing belonged to historians. Schumacher – again – nursed blistered tyres while Ralf chased him but was baulked by slower cars. For the record, this was Schumacher's first win at Hockenheim in a Ferrari and his ninth win of the season, equalling Mansell in 1992 and himself in 1995, 2000 and 2001. *Podium: Schumacher 1h 27m 52s, Montoya @ 10.50s, Ralf Schumacher @ 14.46s.*

BELGIUM, 2002 (Ferrari)

Pole. This was, incidentally, his first at the circuit. He won the race with a minimum of fuss, only Barrichello anywhere near him. Towards the end Brawn told them both to back off to protect their engines. Schumacher now had his tenth win of the season and, incidentally, his sixth at Spa, beating Senna's total of five. Schumacher had now taken pole on all F1 circuits currently in use. *Podium: Schumacher 1h 21m 20.63s, Barrichello @ 1.97s, Montoya @ 18.44s.*

JAPAN, 2002 (Ferrari)

Pole. You know the story, led the whole way in front of Barrichello, the rest in a different race. Schumacher pushed the pace for a couple of laps and, point made, strolled it. The most significant margin at the end wasn't between Schumacher and Barrichello, but both of them back to Räikkönen. By now Formula 1 was in crisis: how much more of this could it take? *Podium: Schumacher 1h 26m 59.69s, Barrichello @ 0.50s, Räikkönen @ 23.29s.*

SAN MARINO, 2003 (Ferrari)

65

Pole. Schumacher earned the admiration of many by winning just hours after the death of his mother. He and Ralf had flown to see her – she was in a coma – on the Saturday night. Ralf, in fact, took the lead and they duelled hard. Ferrari switched to a three-stop strategy. Schumacher had the lead after the first of them and didn't lose it. *Podium: Schumacher 1h 28m 12.05s, Räikkönen @ 1.89s, Barrichello at 2.29.*

SPAIN, 2003 (Ferrari)

66

Pole. Now a youngster, Fernando Alonso in the Renault, challenged Schumacher. Ferrari were running their new car, the F2003-GA, and Formula 1 feared that it might be so good that the season would fall under total Ferrari domination again. Alonso dispelled all that, getting past Barrichello and even leading a couple of laps when Schumacher made his second stop. *Podium: Schumacher 1h 33m 46.93s, Alonso @ 5.71, Barrichello @ 18s.*

AUSTRIA, 2003 (Ferrari)

67

Pole. Schumacher led but a small fire at his pit stop pushed him back to third. He passed Räikkönen at just about the moment Montoya, leading, dropped out with a water leak. He pitted seven laps before Räikkönen and positioned himself so that, when Räikkönen did pit, he swept into the lead again – and held it to the end. Barrichello was a (comparatively) distant third, so there was no question of repeating the 2002 controversy. *Podium: Schumacher 1h 24m 04.88s, Räikkönen @ 3.37s, Barrichello @ 3.95s.*

CANADA, 2003 (Ferrari)

68

Second row. Schumacher finally wrested the championship lead from Räikkönen – who was sixth in the race. Ralf led, Schumacher duelling hard with him although he had brake problems. He resorted to The Tactic: Ralf pitted first and Schumacher did a savagely fast lap before his own stop. Alonso led briefly but, when he pitted, the race fell towards Schumacher. Ferrari saw how much fuel Ralf took on board and gave Schumacher enough to do two more laps. That was decisive. *Podium: Schumacher 1h 31m 13.59s, Ralf Schumacher @ 0.78s, Montoya @ 1.37s.*

ITALY, 2003 (Ferrari)

69

Pole. A consummate victory, bringing his whole season – and the championship – alive again. 'I think,' he said afterwards, 'this is the greatest day of my career.' By Monza, Montoya had bustled and muscled himself into a position where he, not Räikkönen, was the major threat and Schumacher 'made a mistake at the first chicane'. Montoya attacked – they went wheel-to-wheel, 65,000 people holding their breaths – and Schumacher emerged in front. Montoya kept sustained pressure on him until virtually the end. Schumacher didn't make a mistake. *Podium: Schumacher 1h 14m 19.83s, Montoya @ 5.29s, Barrichello @ 11.83s.*

Fourth row. 'I am not clear what was going on, but the car was sliding too much and I could not find any grip.' It rained. 'Tyres played a crucial role. The wet tyres were unbelievable in these conditions.' The early stages of the race were chaotic but, through that, Schumacher moved into the lead and stayed there, imperious in the certainty of his car control. He described the win – taking him to a single point of his sixth World Championship – as important and emotional. *Podium: Schumacher 1h 33m 35.99s, Räikkönen @ 18.26s, Frentzen @ 37.97s.*

Facts of the matter

In his thirteen seasons of Grand Prix racing, Michael Schumacher has won 70 races. Against that, his team-mates have won eleven: Herbert 2, Irvine 2 and Barrichello 7. (Irvine won four for Ferrari in 1999, but two of them were when Schumacher was absent, recovering from a broken leg at Silverstone.)

Expanding on this, Herbert inherited both victories – in 1995 – because Schumacher and Damon Hill crashed when they were up front and it seems unlikely that Herbert would have won either if they hadn't.

When Irvine won in Australia in 1999 Schumacher had a technical problem and started from the back of the grid. He got as high as third before more mechanical problems slowed him.

When Irvine won in Malaysia that same year, Schumacher had returned after the leg injury to help him – Irvine – win the World Championship and twice during the race waited for Irvine to catch him up, and let him go through.

When Barrichello won in Germany in 2000 Schumacher was involved in a crash with Giancarlo Fisichella (Benetton) at the start.

Moreover, Barrichello did not win a single race in 2001 while Schumacher was winning nine. Barrichello did finally begin to get to grips with Schumacher during 2002, winning the European Grand Prix at the Nürburgring after leading throughout (and although Schumacher spun, there is no suggestion he would have overtaken him, or that Ferrari would have imposed team orders).

Barrichello won Hungary from Schumacher, on pole and taking the lead from the lights. Schumacher tracked him

and the final margin – 0.434 seconds – is deceptive because, at the Hungaroring, closing up on the car in front is not the same thing at all as overtaking it. Schumacher said 'in the later stages we were cruising safely to bring the cars home because it is easy to make a mistake here. The reason I did that very quick lap [1m 16.20s on lap 72, beating Barrichello's 1m 16.89s on lap 31] dates back to Silverstone when Rubens was behind me in a similar situation – we were supposed to be going slowly and he suddenly did a quick lap. So today I asked Ross what was the quickest race time and did that lap to pay Rubens back for Silverstone! Our priority is still to get him into second place in the championship. Hopefully, that will come soon and the two of us can have some fun together.'

Something similar happened in the Italian Grand Prix, in that Schumacher seemed content to follow Barrichello, and in the United States they tried to stage a dead-heat, making Barrichello's victory (by 0.011 of a second) largely meaningless.

Barrichello said before the 2003 season that, in career terms, Schumacher had drawn him forward. The evidence for that came at the British Grand Prix where he created a great, inspired, controlled force around himself and nobody could resist it. Schumacher scrabbled around to fourth place: this was perhaps the first time at Ferrari he had been properly out-driven by a team-mate who went on to win.

Suzuka, and the day history surrendered, wasn't the same thing. Barrichello started from pole, Schumacher fourteenth; Barrichello won the race with a highly professional performance. He didn't exactly out-drive Schumacher – he never saw him.

Chapter Nine

THE BIGGEST QUESTION

A life, a career and history itself were compressed into a few seconds one June afternoon in 1979 and, when it was done, Juan-Manuel Fangio signed autographs as if nothing had happened at all.

He'd been driving a Mercedes W125, a pre-War racing car of brutish power, at Donington Park. 'Experiments with higher alcohol content fuels gave a power output of 646bhp at 5800rpm,' wrote Cyril Posthumus. 'Some idea of the enormous potentiality of this new power unit can be gained from the fact that it developed 248bhp at a mere 2000rpm.'[1]

'The designers had developed a machine whose performance would not be surpassed for decades, indeed until 1965. It could be driven at 120kmh [74mph] in first gear, 185 [114] in second, 215 [133] in third and 270 [167] in fourth gear. It could, with special gear ratios, achieve 300kmh [186] and, with aerodynamically developed streamlined bodywork used for record attempts and for racing at Avus [the ultra-fast Berlin circuit] was capable of 400kmh [248].'[2]

Fangio was being presented with a monster.

He had never seen the car or Donington before and hadn't driven in a Grand Prix for two decades. He was aged 68. He wasn't, now, racing the Mercedes but giving a demonstration run[3] and thereby hangs a tale – because, rounding the corner onto the pit lane straight, he fed in too much of that brutish power and hung the tail out, a long way out. He caught that instantaneously. It happened so fast that Nigel Roebuck, covering the event, had barely registered

Schumacher rides the storm in Barcelona, 1996, winning his first race for Ferrari and destroying all opposition. He beat Alesi by 45 seconds, Villeneuve by 48 – and nobody else was even on the same lap when it finished.

that Fangio was in trouble when Fangio had got himself out of trouble 'with almost casual ease'.

Roebuck wrote: 'The next few minutes were unforgettable. As he grew accustomed to car and circuit, Fangio went faster and faster, the slides out of the chicane now anticipated and clearly relished. In the pits, Dan Gurney [an American veteran] like the rest of us was almost unable to believe his eyes, whooping and cheering and clapping his hands. There was spontaneous applause every time around, and on one occasion, after a particularly majestic power slide, Fangio acknowledged it with a bow of his head as he crossed the finish line.'[4]

Fangio won five World Championships between 1951 and 1957, and 24 of the 51 Grands Prix he contested. It remains a staggering strike rate even after all these years.

(As an aside, David Coulthard drove a 1937 W125 at the Mercedes test track at their Stuttgart headquarters in 1997. He was constricted from seeing what the car would really do for reasons of its antiquity and value. In spite of that he made it go fast enough to realise how inadequate by modern standards the brakes were, and was visibly shaken by that when he stopped. He expressed incomprehension that such a car could have been taken round the old Spa circuit at high speed. I include Coulthard's observations because they are interesting in themselves, but more interesting in the light of what Fangio did.)

Barcelona in that storm, and Schumacher cuts cleanly past Villeneuve for the lead.

The biggest question, as Michael Schumacher took his fourth championship in 2001, was twofold: would he go on to equal and then beat Fangio's five titles, and where would his place in history be? With Fangio? With Moss, Clark and Senna, who have long been included whenever the biggest question is asked so that now we truly do have The Famous Five? There is, of course, no unanimity about even this, never mind whether the question can actually be answered. Jo Ramirez – who worked in Grand Prix racing from 1962, latterly as team co-ordinator at McLaren until his retirement at the end of 2001 – says 'for sure I agree with Fangio, Schumacher, Senna, Clark . . . but I'd rather put Stewart and Alain Prost before Moss. Moss could drive

anything and he was brilliant and I liked him enormously but purely in terms of Grand Prix racing I don't think you could put him in front of Alain.'

The reason I put Moss in is that – however intangible, however vague – there is a groundswell of opinion down all these years that he must be in. His brilliance, his car command, his speed, his ability to bring a race to life cannot be doubted. Prost, the technocrat, did not do that. Prost was a minimalist, Moss a life-enhancer.

Younger readers, who have grown up with Schumacher will have heard talk of these great drivers without, perhaps, knowing quite who they were and what they did. Here they are.

CURRICULUM VITAE. Jean-Manuel Fangio, born 24 June 1911, Balcarce, Argentina. He was from a poor family but managed to buy a Model T Ford and raced it. He became so outstanding that he needed the world stage. He first visited Europe in 1948 and drove in Grands Prix from 1950 to 1958 with, as a centrepiece, a victory at the Nürburgring in 1957 after a pit stop went wrong and he had to regain some 50 seconds. He was known as a sportsman and a gentleman. He is the yardstick by which all drivers are measured because he exercised an imperious command of the races. Grand Prix career 1950–1958.

It is, however, a measure of Moss that he finished second in the World Championship in 1955, 1956, 1957 and 1958 and, across the first three of those years, he was beaten by Fangio but was arguably the only man who could push him, certainly on anything approaching a regular basis.

CURRICULUM VITAE. Stirling Moss, born 17 September 1929, London. While accepting that Fangio was a better Grand Prix driver, Moss takes absolute consolation from the knowledge that he was a better sports car driver. Moss prides himself on his 'versatility' – books have been written detailing all the cars he raced. He became synonymous with speed in Britain, and speeding motorists were habitually asked by the traffic police 'who do you think you are, Stirling Moss?' He, too, was a sportsman and a gentleman. Grand Prix career 1951–1961.

I suspected that, from the start of a Grand Prix to the first corner, Moss would cede to no man except Fangio. He said

'it's easier to follow than to lead. Anyway I was quite content to sit behind him to see the way the master did it!' However if they had been in sports cars, 'no way' would Fangio have beaten him. 'That wouldn't have come into the equation.'

CURRICULUM VITAE. Jim Clark, born 4 March 1936, Kilmany, Fifeshire, Scotland. He had an ability so deft and delicate that quantifying it remains elusive. A modest man, he had no idea what it really was. As engine designer Brian Hart says, teams looked at their stop-watches not to know how fast their driver had gone but how far behind Clark he was. Clark only ever drove for Lotus in Formula 1 and his partnership with Colin Chapman, designer genius as well as owner of the team, remains a cornerstone of motor racing history. Grand Prix career 1960–1968.

He and Moss competed against each other in Formula 1 in 1961, Moss's final season.

Senna was always profoundly interested in Clark's career and once, discreetly, went to the museum in Duns, on the Scottish borders, which is dedicated to Clark. He asked the curator what manner of man Clark was – the assembled trophies were of secondary interest. He had plenty of his own.

CURRICULUM VITAE. Ayrton Senna, born 21 March 1960, Sao Paulo, Brazil. He was consumed by the need to win and was *mentally* capable of taking a racing car to its ultimate. I once asked Ken Tyrrell who was the fastest of all the drivers he had seen – nothing to do with any aspect of driving except speed. 'Senna' he said with barely any hesitation. At moments, Senna seemed touched with grace, at others captive to a savage intensity. Grand Prix career 1984–1994.

For the sake of consistency Schumacher is included here in the same format as the other four.

CURRICULUM VITAE. Michael Schumacher, born 3 January 1969, Hürth-Hermülheim, Germany. His early career was good rather than outstanding but he developed carefully, especially with Mercedes in the World Sports Car Championship, to the point where the full range of his abilities could be demonstrated the moment he reached

Formula 1. From then he grew to be monumental. Grand Prix career 1991–present.

Clearly there is no definitive answer to the Biggest Question, but it is legitimate – and perhaps necessary – to ask it, now that Schumacher is slaughtering all manner of records and will clearly slaughter plenty more. Records are a currency in themselves, but not necessarily *the* currency although when they are coming at you with the speed and scale of Schumacher's, you can no longer ignore them. Moreover, merely asking produces instructive (and sometimes provocative) responses.

Here are the words of Stirling Moss. 'Fangio, I suppose, had regularity. In other words, whatever he could do he could do continually. This is an interesting thing. Look at every Grand Prix when it's over: find what pole position had been and notice that the drivers never get to it in the race. In 1961 at Monaco I had pole and if I'd done every lap at that pole pace – the whole hundred laps – I'd only have been 40 seconds quicker than I was.[5] Now it is such a specialised thing.

There are certain drivers out there who are fast but when the race is on they don't do it the same way as qualifying.

'Why I'm using that is to show that whatever Fangio could do, whatever it was, he could do it tomorrow, the day after and the day after that: all the time. Two, he didn't waste any effort. In going round a corner he was precise because he would very rarely ever hang the back out' – which makes the compression at Donington even more remarkable.

'The Goodwood Festival of Speed is very revealing. You have these guys who are amateurs and most of them come round and they are overdoing it. You never saw that with Fangio. He didn't waste any effort. These guys are wasting effort, they're wasting rubber. Fangio was a precise man and Formula 1 in those days, not now, required precision. A fast car at Monaco – look at any picture – would brush the tyres against the barriers. Now they have these chamfered curves and some go here and some go there. . . .'

Jackie Stewart, thrice World Champion, underlines this difference. 'You know, in my entire career I had 17 pole positions. In those days, of course, there were longer practices – sometimes three hours long – and you used those practices to set the car up. And as long as you were up front it was a question of being able to have a car that would race the distance – from a heavy fuel load to a light fuel load, no change of tyres. Ken Tyrrell and I, for example, really did work endlessly on what was the best full race performance car. So pole was nice to have but that was all.'

Schumacher and the Ferrari people also work endlessly on the best race performance and this is what happens when they find it: at the Hungaroring in August 1998, Häkkinen (McLaren) took pole with 1:16.973, Schumacher on the second row with 1:17.366. As the race unfolded, Schumacher found himself running third behind Häkkinen and Coulthard so Brawn decided to change the strategy from two pit stops to three. Famously he told Schumacher over the radio 'you have 19 laps to make up 25 seconds'. Schumacher drove those 19 laps in qualifying mode, although even he could not of course get near his 1:17.366. His best race lap was 1:19.286. With the modern car set up in such different ways for qualifying and race it was intrinsically impossible even for Schumacher to get nearer. What he did do, however, was force the Ferrari down into the 1:19s four times – laps 45, 46, 48 and 54 – and then as he approached the third pit stop he forced this:

Lap 58	1:19.625
Lap 59	1:19.966
Lap 60	1:19.286
Lap 61	1:19.510

Coulthard's best lap was 1:20.546 and Jacques Villeneuve, who finished the race third in the Williams, 1:20.078. Nobody but Schumacher did a lap of 1:19. When he pitted he had gained 26.6 seconds over Coulthard so that he even had a margin over Brawn's demand for 25 seconds. Brawn, one of the most experienced operators in Grand Prix racing, watched this stunned. He says that Schumacher 'doesn't seem to struggle to drive the car on the edge for as long as is necessary. It just doesn't seem to take much out of him mentally or physically.'

The timeless theme is that, in their circumstances, Fangio and Moss were faster than anybody else competing against them, so was Stewart, and Senna had so much speed in qualifying that it scattered a generation of opponents. Schumacher was not flamboyant about such matters but, at the Hungaroring, he proved beyond reasonable doubt that he could have run with them.

Nor is it simply a matter of drawing up a short list – The Famous Five – and relegating the rest to the second division. 'All I've ever said, and I sincerely believe it is the correct way to look at it, is this: all we *can* look at is who was the undisputed leader of the era in which that person lived,' Stewart says. 'Fangio was the undisputed leader however good Farina was or Ascari was. There was no doubt that Fangio was the regular winner. He moved teams and cars as he saw fit to match his talents. So if it was Ferrari or Maserati or Mercedes-Benz or whoever he drove for, he would flip-flop them all the time to get the best. Enzo Ferrari hated him because of that. Ferrari expected loyalty but he never gave loyalty back. If you go from Fangio, the next real leader was Jim Clark. That combination of Colin Chapman and Jim Clark was unbeatable and however good Graham Hill was or Jack Brabham or Dan Gurney and everybody else, at that time Jim Clark was the undisputed leader.

'Maybe I was that next one and then there was Niki, who dominated the mid-1970s, and then there was unquestionably Prost, and then Senna and now Schumacher.'

Broadening that, 'nobody knows if, say, Jean-Claude Killy's record of Olympic gold medals in the giant slalom, the slalom and the downhill will ever be done again because it is now a different build of man, a different race of man [in ski racing, where the events have their specialists].[6] So you would *only* look at the time when Michael Schumacher lived, and you'd say he was the best. To start trying to wave a wand and conjure magical visions and see Schumacher in a car and Fangio and Clark or

Of course drivers can't show their versatility these days, can they? Schumacher gets the Renault Clio almost onto two wheels at the Schumachers' kart track at Kerpen, near Cologne. Weber, who must have seen all this before, sits it out. The US Grand Prix 2001, and Schumacher says farewell to Jo Ramirez (right), a friend to the whole of Formula 1 for three decades and a backbone of the McLaren team.

anybody else with him is for nobody to judge because it can't be done.'

In the absolute sense, you cannot argue with this but I intend to push the idea further because it gets more intriguing.

Straight away we must confront a fundamental difference between yesterday and today. The versatility which Moss holds so dear, and which seems to argue the full range – and therefore quality – of a driver, is almost unavailable now. Moss says 'the rules stop that because the drivers have allowed the rules – or the organisers and team owners have made the rules – that you can't race more than one car in a day. They can't do a curtain-raiser in a touring car or a sports car. In my day you not only had all that lot, you had the Race of Champions[7] and we raced in that for nothing.

'I drove right across the board and I think it is a very important thing. I know from other people I meet, people of my era, that they enjoyed being able to race against the top Formula 1 drivers in saloon or sports cars. People say "I

raced against you in some race somewhere" and I think that is part of it. And I was very lucky. My career was following the war when there weren't the established stars. I hadn't got to knock anybody down – unlike now when anybody coming in will have to knock Michael off the top. I was lucky I didn't have that.'

Well, Moss had Fangio but never mind. . . .

Accepting that the modern driver cannot brandish a Curriculum Vitae anything like that of Moss, there *are* examples, however sparse and sometimes unsatisfactory, of this versatility. For example, the following Grand Prix drivers have won the Le Mans 24-hour sports car race since 1990: Martin Brundle, Bertrand Gachot, Johnny Herbert, Derek Warwick, Yannick Dalmas, Mark Blundell, Mauro Baldi, JJ Lehto, Alexander Wurz, Michele Alboreto, Stefan Johansson, Pierluigi Martini and Emanuele Pirro.

When Schumacher drove Le Mans with the Mercedes team in 1991 he was partnered by Karl Wendlinger and Fritz Kreutzpointner, making his sports car début, as we saw in

Chapter 2. None had seen Le Mans before but Schumacher set fastest lap (3:35.564, an average of 141mph/226kph) which a contemporary report describes as 'stunning'. Wendlinger crashed the car and they finished fifth.

That season Schumacher drove in seven other rounds of the World Sports Car Championship, taking a second place at Silverstone and, partnered by Frentzen, winning Autopolis in Japan. Schumacher took the first stint, moving up from sixth on the grid and cutting inside Warwick to be third at Turn One. By lap nine he was with the leaders and took Teo Fabi (Jaguar) on the *outside* of Turn One. The leading car dropped out with oil pressure problems and Schumacher had the win. 'I'm really happy for myself, but more for the team. They have done such a big work this year it's unbelievable. To keep all the time the motivation to continue like this, it was really hard.'

Sound familiar?

As a curious historical footnote, Fangio, Moss and Clark competed at Le Mans but never won it. Senna, who never went there, did however compete in a round of the World Sports Car Championship with the Joest team at the Nürburgring in 1984. As a complete stranger to the team and the car he did a fast lap in the wet and then, reputedly, asked what all the dials on the dashboard meant! The car, a Porsche 956, had mechanical problems in the race although the team owner, Reinhold Joest, adored Senna overtaking another car on the outside – and was astonished when, after the race, Senna came to him with a long list of ways he felt the car could be improved.

Incidentally, Moss says that the difference between Formula 1 and sports cars is 'rather like writing with a very fine nib, which is Formula 1, or the broad nib, which is the sports car. It's much easier to make your writing look good with a broad nib. Moreover, Formula 1 was always where the line between right and wrong was very, very fine.' Surveying it, there can be no doubt that these great ones could write both ways, and virtually at will.

In May 1984 Senna competed in a race of Mercedes 190Es – the saloon car – to inaugurate the new Nürburgring. The celebrity entry included Lauda, Rosberg, John Watson, Denny Hulme, Scheckter, James Hunt, Jack

Brabham, John Surtees and Moss. The drivers regarded it as fun, all except for Senna who, Watson believes, saw it as a chance to advance his career by winning, and did win (from Lauda). Senna once spent a day in mid-Wales driving a variety of rally cars on the equivalent of a special stage and, by close of play, had adapted to the point where he was making them go fast.

There is no comparison between this, of course, and what Jim Clark did, entering the RAC Rally, taking Lotus Cortinas round Brands Hatch, mostly on two wheels, and winning Indianapolis.

Historian Doug Nye suggests that Clark, who he met, was 'curious to know' what various sorts of cars would do and, when he had found out, his curiosity was satisfied. This may have been why he accepted an invitation to drive a 1936 ERA racing car during the French Grand Prix meeting at Rouen in 1962.

Gregor Grant in *Autosport* wrote: 'Jim Clark was persuaded to try Patrick Lindsey's ERA He turned in three laps, and shook everyone by getting down to 2 mins 48.7 secs, a really splendid time for such a veteran machine.' Nye says Clark hardly used the brakes, simply slaloming through the corners.

Schumacher's demonstration run at Silverstone 2001 in the 1961 Ferrari . . .

Pole for the Grand Prix was taken by Clark in the Lotus at 2m 9.6s, so that – over the 4.06 mile course – he was not absurdly slower in the pre-War sit-up-and-beg car!

In the Golden Age Motor Race at the meeting (10 laps) Lindsey won in the ERA and set a fastest lap of 2m 50s – more than two seconds slower than Clark, who of course had never driven the car before. (Nye points out, however, that Clark's time was set after qualifying, the Golden Age was on race day when the weather was very different *and* there was oil on the track. This does not in any way diminish Nye's regard for Clark – a 'genius', and he uses that word for Schumacher as well. 'What they have is what 99.99% of the rest of the world does not have. What is it? Well, whatever it is it defies rational analysis.')

Jim Endruweit was a Lotus mechanic at Rouen. 'We were not unnaturally fairly busy with our own business getting ready for the Grand Prix. The owner of the ERA contacted Jimmy – came to see him or whatever – with the outcome that Jimmy was going to drive this car. I probably didn't even know it was an ERA! Jimmy drove it and the owner was standing there sweating a bit. Jimmy bimbled by – drove past looking very relaxed – on his first lap, and he was quick, next lap he was quicker. He did a time that the owner thought was out of this world, couldn't believe. Jimmy brought it in and the car was fine, it wasn't even sweating. It seemed remarkable that he could get into – or onto – such a vehicle and drive it amazingly quickly without flogging it. How did Jimmy take that? As far as I know, he didn't think he had done anything remarkable. "Yeah, that was fine, I enjoyed that." He was tremendously relaxed about that sort of stuff.'

I asked Jo Ramirez why Clark was so much better than others of his era? 'Like Schumacher and Senna, they are just born with it. They didn't have to work hard at it at all. I regret about modern Grand Prix racing that you don't see the drivers driving anything else. One of the greatest things was watching Jim Clark in the Lotus Cortina round Brands on two wheels and lapping a second and a half quicker than anybody else. He'd have the nearside wheel above the grass and the other wheel just touching the apex of the corner, and the car just about to roll. You'd think *he will roll, he must roll* – but he didn't. He was idolised by all the other drivers.' Ramirez adds a tantalising postscript. Those same drivers thought 'if Clark could do it, it can be done'. Not by them though.

One test of true greatness is how drivers exploit treacherous conditions when those around them can't. In Spain in 1992 Schumacher, still inexperienced, pushed Nigel Mansell hard. . . .

Jackie Stewart concedes that the great ones have always been versatile 'but that changed and is no longer the case. For example, one or two of the guys go and drive a touring car against the top drivers there – say in Germany – it's always tough for them to dominate in that. Some people in the old days could. I remember winning four races on the same day at Crystal Palace in four different racing cars – you might go from a Formula 3 car to a Lotus Elan to an E-Type Jaguar.

'In Michael's case that hasn't shown up for a while. Since he left sports cars with Mercedes you haven't seen him apart from one or two karting events, and he drove at Silverstone. What I'm saying is that today the specialist lives, the generalist is no longer there. That makes it a very narrow band that these guys work in.'

We've already seen how Schumacher handled Tambay's 1983 turbo Ferrari and how, like a very modern man, his thoughts were dominated by safety – a precise reflection of the world he grew up in and no reflection on his ability. At Silverstone in 2001, he took part in a commemoration of Ferrari's first Grand Prix victory – there – on 14 July 1951. An engineer who worked on the car that day, Ener Vecchi, was present to see Schumacher take the car (which evidently he'd said would need work done on its brakes!) for a demonstration run. The car was described as the 'sister' of the one Froilan Gonzalez won in. Schumacher said 'to drive it is an absolute pleasure' and he made it go a bit on the straights.

No doubt any competent driver could have done the same. The point I'm trying to establish is much broader: however fragmentary the evidence, it implies that Senna and Schumacher would have been formidable driving the wide variety of cars which Clark, Moss and Fangio did; that they were not just robotic specialists cushioned by technology. If you accept that then you can approach The Biggest Question now that The Famous Five are competing with equal equipment, as the saying goes.

NOTES

[1] *The Racing Car*, C. Clutton, C. Posthumus and D. Jenkinson (Batsford, 1962)

[2] *The Complete History of Grand Prix Motor Racing*, Adriano Cimarosti (Aurum, 1997).

[3] As part of the Gunnar Nilsson Memorial Trophy Race Meeting.

[4] *Autosport*, 7 June 1979.

[5] In 1961, Moss took pole at Monaco with a lap of 1:39.1 and by mid-point in the race was below that (1:38.6) before he set joint fastest lap at 1:36.3 on lap 85.

[6] At the Winter Olympics in Grenoble, 1968, Killy won the downhill, the slalom and the giant slalom. Then the specialists came. Even four years later, at Sapporo, different ski-racers won each of the three events.

[7] A non-Championship Formula 1 race run from 1965 to 1983 at Brands Hatch.

Facts of the matter

A measure of a driver's capabilities is how he performs in wet races, because the most delicate car control and sensitivity are needed. Here are the wet races of The Five. They are not intended to be comparative because, by definition, a race run on the old Spa – Belgian country roads, uneven cambers, trees, ditches, houses – in a car with narrow tyres during a thunderstorm was a different creature to one run on wide, wet-weather tyres round the new Spa during light rain. What these paragraphs *do* demonstrate is how good each of The Five was, and how few mistakes they made. Note how few crashes there are. I have not adhered to any strict definition of a wet race (one officially designated so) but, rather, included all races where it rained – even if that was a shower.

FANGIO: Switzerland 1951, first; Britain 1953, second; Argentina 1954, first; France 1954, first; Britain 1954, fourth; Holland 1955, first; Belgium, 1956, did not finish, transmission; Italy 1956, eighth.

MOSS: Switzerland 1951, eighth; Belgium 1952, engine failed on lap 1; Holland 1952, engine failed on lap 74 when seventh; Britain 1954, rear axle failed on lap 81 when second; Holland 1955, second; Belgium 1956, lost wheel; Italy 1956, first; Monaco 1960, first; Britain 1961, had been as high as second, brake pipe failed on lap 45; Germany 1961, first.

CLARK: Britain 1961, oil leak on lap 63 when fifth; Germany 1961, fourth; Germany 1962, fourth; Belgium 1963, first; France 1963, first; Belgium 1965, first; Belgium 1966, engine failed on lap 1; Britain 1966, fourth; Germany 1966, accident on lap 12; Canada 1967, ignition failed on lap 70 when leading.

SENNA: Monaco 1984, second; Portugal 1985, first; Belgium 1985, first; Britain 1988, first; Germany 1988, first; Japan 1988, first; Canada 1989, seventh; Belgium 1989, first; Australia 1989, crashed when leading; Canada 1990, first; Brazil 1991, first; San Marino 1991, first; Spain 1991, fifth; Australia 1991, first; Spain 1992, spun on lap 63 when third; Belgium 1992, fifth; Brazil 1993, first;

Steps through the storms. In Brazil in 1993 (above) he drove prudently to third place while cars spun off everywhere. This (above right) is his pit stop in that race: easy does it. Moving through standing water (right).

Europe 1993, first; San Marino 1993, hydraulics failure after 42 laps when second.

SCHUMACHER: Australia 1991, collision after 5 laps when fifth; Spain 1992, second; Belgium 1992, first; Brazil 1993, third; Europe 1993, crash on lap 23 when fifth; San Marino 1993, second; Canada 1994, first; Japan 1994, second; Belgium 1995, first; Europe 1995, first; Japan 1995, first; Brazil 1996, third; Monaco 1996, crashed on the first lap; Spain 1996, first; Belgium 1996, first; Monaco 1997, first; France 1997, first; Belgium 1997, first; Britain 1998, first; Belgium 1998, crash on lap 26 when leading; France 1999, fifth; Europe 2000, first; Canada 2000, first; Belgium 2000, second; Japan 2000, first; Malaysia 2001, first; Brazil 2001, second; Britain 2002, first; Brazil, 2003, crash on lap 26 when third; Indianapolis, first.

Jim Endruweit was at the Nürburgring with Clark and Lotus in 1962. 'It was a dreadful race, atrocious weather. Jimmy was on the front row and fluffed the start – I think his engine stalled – and he went off at the back of the field. He worked his way up – Dan Gurney, Graham Hill and John Surtees occupying the first three places – and caught them from being four *minutes* behind or whatever.

When he reached fourth he stayed there. When he came in we were talking about it and he said "well, I frightened myself a bit" and he backed off to the same speed as the leaders. He was almost in cruising mode as he did that, and on The Ring in that weather it was unbelievable. He normally didn't drive that fast. No matter what he was doing he virtually always had something in hand.' (The Nürburgring was 22.7km/14.1m but even so Clark overtook either 15 or 16 cars on the opening lap. On lap 11 of the 15, according to one account[1] 'the car went into a horribly long slide and counter-slide, and Clark decided to ease up.')

Certainly Stirling Moss feels that Schumacher is 'exceptionally good, yes, but so was Senna. The great ones all are, of course. You have to be. That's what makes some great and the others very good.'

When Senna won the European Grand Prix at Donington in 1993, his performance in changing weather conditions was so overwhelming – at one point he led by a whole lap – that Jo Ramirez could not believe it. 'Mega, absolutely mega. That was the race that showed the world how good he was, especially those first two laps.'

Could Schumacher have driven those two laps?

'I think no, but I'd also say I'm biased. He's immensely quick in the wet, but. . . .'

What is it that they have?

'They feel the car so much better than the rest and that

enables them to anticipate much better too. The only one of those great drivers who wasn't so good in the wet was Alain Prost. In Alain's mind was the visibility: in the wet it's very, very hard to see. He never forgot that he and one of his great mates, Didier Pironi, crashed at Hockenheim in the wet. It wasn't Alain's fault but he felt bad, and Pironi never drove again. Prost said it could happen to anybody. Then there was the race in Adelaide where Alain refused to start, and Ayrton hit Brundle – but on the side of Brundle's car, so he lost a wheel. If he'd hit full, then maybe he would have lost his legs. Who knows?'

Ross Brawn has already discussed this feel, although in a more general way. 'We do a lot of reaction training for the starts and Michael's reaction to a light going off is not particularly special. Obviously his reactions to the feel of the car are incredible. It's a feel for what all four tyres are doing and when they've reached the limit of the car. It shows in the fact that he is very quick on the first lap out of the pits. All the other drivers take four or five laps. That's where his talent is most obvious.'

Both Senna and Schumacher had innate skill in the wet from near the beginning of their careers. Senna, competing in a Formula Ford 1600 race at Thruxton, was so fast that Dennis Rushen, co-owner of a Formula 2000 team, went immediately to him afterwards and offered him a drive for the following season at a reduced rate.

Schumacher, competing in a German Formula Ford race at Salzburg, was so fast that Josef Kaufmann, owner of a Formula 3 team, went immediately to him afterwards and offered him a drive for the following season. Kaufmann remembers 'he ran sixth or seventh and worked his way up. To be able to do that is not normal with only a little Formula Ford experience. He'd only done a few races.'

This *feel* seems inborn, not learnt, and if you have it you always have it – if you don't, you never will. Pat Symonds reflects on Schumacher's victory in Spain in the Ferrari in 1996 when, starting third, he almost stalled. From there he rode the storm – visibility in the spray was so bad that he was unaware of how many cars he'd overtaken on the opening lap – and won by 45 seconds.

'You take it as read that he has an incredible natural ability to drive the car. That, to me, is plainly obvious. I think there are other people who have similar abilities to drive a car fast – you can even argue that some may have greater abilities, but they didn't have the complete package. Some of the things that Nigel [Mansell] could do with a car were astounding. Arguably some of them were better than anything Michael's done – but Michael doesn't need to do those things. . . .'

NOTE [1] *The German Grand Prix*, Cyril Posthumus (Temple Press Books, 1966).

Chapter Ten

LESSONS OF HISTORY

'I always relate it to a Sunday afternoon just before 2pm and the race,' Gary Anderson says. 'Take all the Formula 1 drivers, line them up and ask them why they're there. Most of them will look at you gormlessly because they don't *really* know – but Michael does, and even when he was first in the racing car he knew what he was doing, no doubt of that. It's all about getting your head straight and making sure you know. Michael has his head straight. Come 2 o'clock on the Sunday afternoon Michael isn't yapping and shouting and mooching around, he's enjoying himself at being serious.

'People criticise him for his dedication and commitment and all sorts of stuff but they're just jealous, really, because they can't see how important it is. His whole fitness is incredible, for instance. I have seen him in Brazil at six o'clock on a Sunday morning: we're leaving for the track and he's coming back from a run. How many drivers are up at 6am on a Sunday, never mind having a run to loosen themselves up a bit?'

These are formidable words portraying, as they do, a formidable man.

Stirling Moss approaches it from a different direction. 'Jimmy was a racer. One doesn't think of him particularly as a racer but he was. The whole of my career, which was 529 races, I drove against a lot of names, against a lot of fantastic drivers, but only about three or four *racers*.' The words tumble from Moss, precise, urgent. Yes, he will say, Fangio, was a racer too.[1]

So what is it that makes the racer as against the very good driver?

Indianapolis 2000, and the United States rediscovers Formula 1 just as Formula 1 rediscovers the United States. Coulthard (left) is about to seize the lead from Schumacher – but he won't be able to keep it.

'Character. What makes one man brave and another man a coward? Why are certain people born with certain attitudes and attributes? My wife is so honest that if I left a diary on the table she wouldn't read it. I would. What makes that difference? Genes, I suppose. I know a guy who ran some stores in the Bahamas and who drove in the speed weekend there[2]. If he had turned his mind to it he could have been a bloody good racer, and I could tell that, not by seeing how he drove but by knowing the person. You see the same in business. There are people who become leaders because that's the way they are. With racers it's no different.

'Graham Hill was exceptionally good: he did more with less talent than any person I can think of, but Graham was not a racer. Graham was an exceptionally good driver in the way that Prost was one of the great drivers, Jackie Stewart another. I don't think these guys were racers. They were fantastic drivers but you have to realise there is a difference. Racers are guys who go out there and bloody well race. "Boy, I'm not going to let you win." That is a mentality: your car might be incapable of winning but you never think in those terms. Schumacher is the same, Ayrton was the same.'

Schumacher starts sixteenth on the grid at Spa. He does not say to himself 'I might as well go home.' He thinks 'how long will it take me to get into the lead?'

'That is the sign of a great racer. He is a person who has sufficient of that to bring him up to the top. Fangio to me was the most difficult one of all, even more difficult than Jimmy, to quantify. With Fangio it may have been that I couldn't speak to him in his own language.[3] Another thing about the great ones: their career graphs go up at a constant rate from the beginning and go up quickly. There are no plateaux as you get with other drivers. They are always going up.'

Moss has neatly separated those he rates the sloggers (Hill) and the technicians (Stewart, Prost) from those few who have quite different basic instincts and obey the phrase *motor race* in its literal sense, everything subordinated to that.[4]

Schumacher's got a wife and two kids, more money than you can shake a stick at, but if you put him into a pressure point he doesn't back off. If it's you and he going towards La Source hairpin . . . .

'. . .I know I'm going to beat him out of it. . . .'

. . .he's not going to back off.

'That's when it's interesting, that's when you come to the situation where you say "I don't bloody well care whether you're Schumacher or not, sod you. No way will you come out first."'

But he's looking across at you saying 'Stirling Moss, sod YOU.'

'No, no, he'll know by the time we go into the corner that I'm going to come out first.'

How?

'Because . . . because it's my business to make him know.'

What if he thinks it's his business to make you know?

'I'll prove him wrong.'

And that's the mind of the racer?

'Yeah. The great thing about racing is the human person. You can test how strong a piece of metal is, you know when it's going to break, but you don't with the human mind. If your life depended on holding onto a bar, how long could you hold it? Now how long could you hold it because your wife is at risk? You can't quantify people. If motor racing is your choice, and you are an extraordinary person, you'll find ways of turning the wick up a bit because it's necessary. That happens.

'I knew there were times when I drove much faster than I'd normally drive. You get to the end of the race and think "Christ, that *was* quick. How did I get there?" You go round a corner, it's just absolutely right and you carry that thing through. You get this rhythm going and it's a rhythm that you don't necessarily have when you're driving fast. If you're lucky – which usually doesn't happen – you click in and you find that it flows, and suddenly the things that were doubtful before are just natural now.

'That is personality, because the difference in speed between Michael Schumacher and even a moderately good driver is not that much – but it is enormous when you try and make it up. That's the point. A tenth of a second isn't long but you try to gain a tenth of a second. It's enormous. And it gets more enormous when you are of his stature because he's *always* there, always right on it.'

Juan-Manuel Fangio and Stirling Moss (top left) are interviewed by actor James Garner at Long Beach in 1976. All discussions about greatness have to begin with Fangio and Moss. All discussions about greatness have to move on to Jim Clark, here (above right) in France in 1967 with Keith Duckworth (of Cosworth fame) and Graham Hill. Clark seemed to be able to make the Lotus caress a circuit so lightly (above) that, for example, his tyre wear was minimal, and exactly the same on all four tyres. Even tyre technicians found this difficult to believe.

Jackie Stewart is on this same theme. 'Senna very seldom seemed to drive within the car. If you want to look back, and I certainly have, at all the footage of Senna's laps versus Prost's laps when they had on-board cameras, Prost's movement of the steering wheel was at least 50% less than Senna's. Senna was bullying the car everywhere whereas Prost was coaxing it.'

But you were a coaxer.

'Which I think is the best. Jim Clark was a coaxer. Let's talk about the guys with the real heads: Lauda was a clinical thinker, Prost was The Professor, I was a little bit the same way – clinical and analytical about what I did. Jim drove Colin Chapman's cars because he trusted Colin.'

But Clark comes to us as a man who was so naturally gifted that he didn't have to think about it.

'He didn't, but having said that, how do you account for the number of victories he had? I know he drove the best car at the best time, but most of us [the great ones] did. Jimmy had a wonderful car because Chapman was such an extraordinary person. Jim knew how fast to drive – and how slow to drive.'

Old masters . . . Fangio in 1976 (left) driving the Mercedes W196 from the mid-1950s. Moss in 1977 driving the Maserati 250F, also from the 1950s.

Schumacher is a coaxer.

'Not like Clark, Prost or even myself. When Schumacher sets his car up I would say the brain of his car is over the front wheels. You see him going into a corner: he turns in very late and very sharp. Now that's partly to do with today's technology but, even so, the brain would be much further forward in his car than it would be in Häkkinen's or Coulthard's – I don't know about Montoya yet.'

In Schumacher's hot qualifying laps you don't feel subtlety.

'But you didn't feel it with Senna either. Senna didn't have the same subtlety as Prost.' Stewart adds: 'All of them have got big minds.'

Moss, incidentally, says that Senna was the greatest racer he saw. I put that to Jo Ramirez who worked with Senna for the six seasons Senna was at McLaren. 'I think so, yes. Ayrton hated to be second. That's what eventually took his life – because he *had* to stay in front.'

Moss is not suggesting that he would have run Schumacher off the track to win *La Source*, of course, and for

two reasons. Drivers in the 1950s and 1960s wouldn't have survived long in the cars of that time if they did, and people didn't behave like that anyway. 'Consider that Senna and Prost, two of the greatest drivers who have ever lived, both drove each other off the road – or tried to – at 170 miles an hour. I am convinced that if they had driven in my era they wouldn't have done it. It's not just that they'd probably have got killed, it's that it just wasn't the done thing. I think if Schumacher had raced with us he would have driven with the ethics of people of our era.'

Modern safety, and perhaps modern competitiveness, have led Schumacher to do alarming things to protect his lead from the start to the equivalent of *La Source* everywhere, once moving so far over on brother Ralf that closing your eyes was a good idea. I watch film of old races, black and white newsreel stuff, and the rush from the start line is always a flurry of cars travelling in straight lines, looking for advantage but never weaving for position. Then, with a certain decorum, they filter into the first corner one at a time, single file.

In that sense, Schumacher is the opposite. Winning is all, the ethics of sport lost somewhere back there before the mega money, the hype, the television and the PR industry got hold of it and twisted it into, frequently, an ugly thing. Before, in fact, Formula 1 became a cash dispenser. I put it to Moss that we don't really have ethics in the traditional sense at all and he replied 'no, we don't'. Of course Fangio and Moss and Clark wanted to win, but not to the degree of, say, Senna who, after he crashed at Monaco in 1988, was still crying in his apartment when Ramirez rang him *that night*.

'The attitude that Ayrton had, that will to win, he had in go-karts when he was a kid in Brazil, and it lasted all the way to Tamburello,' Ramirez says. 'Schumacher would have had the same when he was in karts. Damon Hill had to really work at this, it didn't come easy to Damon. Alain Prost was so smooth that we used to say to him "tell us when you're doing your quick lap so we'll know which one it is!" Prost had a very different style, not only in the car but out of it. He was very quiet. Ayrton had this will. . . .'

Few doubt that Schumacher has it too, and when he ran into the back of David Coulthard at Spa in the wet in 1998

he detonated. He stormed down the pit lane to confront Coulthard with a wild look about him and had to be restrained. Impossible to imagine Fangio, Moss or Clark doing that – but not Senna. However, like Senna, Schumacher has mellowed with the years to the point where he can drive a whole season with only occasional outrages and controversies.

Moss echoes Stewart's stricture about asking The Biggest Question. 'I don't think you can compare one man in one era with another. It's difficult enough in athletics – Roger Bannister with a miler now[5] – but at least they are running the same distance with virtually the same equipment. In motor racing the eras are quite different. Those of us who overlapped from one era into another obviously made the change without too much difficulty – it was a seamless change – but to take Fangio, Nuvolari or whoever and try them in a modern car isn't feasible. However I believe that if Fangio had raced now he'd have been the same as he was then.'

That's why, with all respect to Moss, I'm pursuing The Question and Schumacher's place in it. You might think, too, that The Five would have shared characteristics.

'That's the most difficult thing I find: not if you look at them physically, not if you look at the way they talk and so on, but inside there must be a common denominator,' Moss says. 'What makes a man a racer – which is what we're talking about – isn't really connected to speed as much as it is to personality. The difference in going round a corner between any of those would be absolutely minimal. In fact it's usually minimal in the top three in any era, but when the chips are down – and you start to talk about a race, passing back markers, when you're going to do *this*, when you're going to do *that* – all those things fall in place. They make him the racer. When I go into a corner with

another guy I don't have a doubt, there can't be a doubt, you have to have complete faith. If you are in any doubt you're not a racer.

'The other interesting thing is that you don't find in those people any big-headedness about it. Today the moderate drivers have to convince themselves that they are as good as they think they are. Schumacher doesn't, of course he doesn't. He is that good, and that's the point. It's confidence, not being big-headed.'

Fangio and Moss were gentlemen, Clark was almost painfully shy, Senna understood (and talked of) humility, and Schumacher seems to have his head straight. Have you ever heard any of them boasting?

You might imagine that self-doubt would be completely absent but Stewart does not agree. 'Jim Clark had a lot of self-doubt. I did too. I always thought people were better than I was and it was a question of me having to try harder. Out of a racing car Jimmy couldn't make a decision to save himself. When it was about a girlfriend, when it was about where to go for dinner, when it was about whether to go to a movie, he would not be able to decide.'

I remember you said you were right in the middle of Florida somewhere, Clark driving, and you stopped at a railway line, nothing for a thousand miles each way, and he said 'do you think we should go across?'

'He said "what do you think?" It was single track too! But when he got into a car he drove it with natural skill and mind-management. I don't think he had self-doubts in a racing car, but everything to deal with before getting into the car he had.'

Jo Ramirez gives an anecdote about how ordinary Clark was outside a racing car. 'I first came over [from Mexico] in 1962. I planned to drive but that didn't happen, although I

The saddest day, when the leadership was passed on from Senna to Schumacher. Imola, 1 May 1994: the start of the San Marino Grand Prix (above), Senna on pole. The re-start (right), Senna gone – forever.

got involved in Grand Prix racing. I became the go-for at Ferrari. There was no way they were going to give me a proper job because I was not Italian and I didn't speak Italian and I had no qualifications! We'd go to the races on the Continent by boat across the Channel. Clark would be on it. We'd sit in the bar and play cards quite normally, because that's the way it was.'

Before we look at specific qualities, Moss explains why we are talking about so few drivers. 'If you take the greatest singers in the world you've only got three or four, if you take the greatest jugglers in the world you've only got three or four, in every era you never have more than four at most. I think if I'd been more intelligent I could have made a bigger mark – if I'd joined up with factory teams earlier and gone where the main chance was, as Fangio did.'

In that sense, Fangio was very modern indeed.

One common characteristic is that the great drivers have time when they travel at racing speed because to them it is happening slowly. As Jim Endruweit puts it, 'you get the strong impression that Schumacher is driving at, well, nine-tenths.'

I pursued that with Ramirez.

Did you notice that Ayrton had this ability to drive a car 100% but using only 90% of himself, so that he had 10% spare – like Schumacher?

'They do seem to have that.'

It has to mean, and this is where it gets almost scary, that for most of their career they are driving faster than anybody else but nowhere near their own limit.

'Very true. For example, let me speak about the gismos – active suspension, ride heights and all of that. On the straight Ayrton used to be able to raise the car for maximum speed and lower it for the corner. When he told Gerhard Berger that – because there was a difference in lap times – Gerhard said "bloody hell, you've time to do that?"

It was the difference between Ayrton and the rest. Schumacher seems very cool, he doesn't get excited about it. David Coulthard is like that on the radio. Ayrton was excitable, but that was his way.

'You could talk to Ayrton about everything. He was so quick to think and grasp things. Working with him you learned about life.'

Stewart once gave an extraordinary description of how he treated his mind as a balloon and, holding that mental picture, deliberately deflated it. I wondered if he – and Schumacher – can think slowly?

'Yes, of course. God had given me a talent which would allow things to be viewed slowly. Speed didn't exist. A lot of people are not synchronised. How would you like to be receiving a service from Pete Sampras? It would just be a blur of fluff to me. Take Mohammad Ali. He seldom got hit because he saw the punch coming almost from the ankle to the knee to the weight distribution his opponents made for the arm going back, whereas for me it would have been a

blur again, and then hospital. But when I was driving a racing car I had all the time in the world to see everything that was required, not just to come off the gas pedal – although coming off the gas pedal was in itself an art whilst not disturbing the car's forward motion to a point where the pitch changed. Nobody ever told me anything about that: it was learning from experience.

'What happens in life – I don't care what it is – is that first of all you have to get experience. It doesn't matter how much natural talent you've got. From experience you gain some knowledge. When you have experience and knowledge you can sometimes accomplish things.

'People talk about reactions but it's somewhat overstated to say *you've got such fast reactions*. It's got nothing to do with the muscular response to any particular situation, it is the consumption of information which that person is getting from his eyes or ears or hands or whatever.'

A television programme in 2001 showed drivers' reactions tested: a piece of paper was dropped without warning and they had to catch it by clapping their hands. Schumacher was no quicker at this than the others.

'Right, correct, and that's what I'm saying, but now consider what would happen if you put a few other elements into it. Suppose Schumacher had had to chew gum and walk at the same time as catching the paper. You would have seen him take the lead comfortably. That would be the difference.'

I put it to Ramirez that, without being provocative, Prost didn't have what Senna had in the same way that Häkkinen hasn't got what Schumacher has – a merciless hardness of purpose.

'I think,' Ramirez replied after a long pause for thought, 'one of the things Ayrton had and Schumacher has is this racecraft. They were so much cleverer in being able to pace their own race. You watch Schumacher do a pit stop: he comes in at the last moment, comes quick, gets out quick, doesn't lose any time at all. I remember the Hungarian Grand Prix and it was just unbelievable. They told him on the radio 'you can win if you stop three times – so you can have the car light – but you have to do 19 qualifying laps. And he did it. *Nineteen laps at qualifying speed.* Only once did he have the car sideways, and he never lost it. Ayrton could have done those laps.'

The great ones have 10% left for when they need it.

'They can just turn this on like a tap.'

How? What is that?

'They have their own special limits. For example, Mika hasn't got this racecraft that Schumacher has. Mika needs to have the character to keep pushing all the time. We had Michael Andretti and when he went away Mika came in at Estoril for the Portuguese Grand Prix [in 1993]. Ayrton had let his guard down, thought this young guy was no competition and Mika outqualified him. I remember at the drivers' meeting Mika had a smile from ear to ear and Gerhard said "I bet you that as long as you live you will never ever beat him again." We went to the Japanese Grand

Prix after Portugal and Alain was on pole, Senna second and Mika third. In the race Mika was so far behind Ayrton at the end that it meant he was almost a second a lap slower. Mika knew he'd had absolutely no problem with the car, it was fantastic, but he could not reproduce his qualifying for lap after lap in the race.'

Stewart insists that the leaders in each generation have 'not only been given a natural gift from God – it is certainly not their own doing – but as they sharpen their skills they have also recognised that the single most important thing of all is man management, of how to manicure and massage the talent to a higher level. Now take somebody of immense talent, for example Chris Amon.[6] He had as much if not more skill than many of the top Grand Prix drivers of that day, but he chose the wrong cars with the wrong people. Schumacher wouldn't have done that: he'd only drive for the best. I wouldn't have done it either.

'Some people are natural ball-catchers. Some people are natural golfers or tennis players. They have got what it takes to do that. There is no doubt that Tiger Woods has a particular talent, and Nick Faldo had it, so did Palmer and Nicklaus. In the same way Picasso wasn't a manufactured artist. Neither was Matisse. These are people who have *it*. What did Laurence Olivier have? Something more than everybody else. You could say Gene Kelly had more mind-management than natural talent whereas Fred Astaire had the most wonderful fluidity about his dancing, and that was because he was just so naturally gifted.'

One of the central aspects is whether driving a Grand Prix car is more difficult now than then, something about which Lauda has no doubt. He drove a modern car not so long ago and found the traction control and paddle gearchanging made life much easier.

Nigel Stepney echoes that. At the end of the 2001 season, as we have seen, Schumacher had 43 pole positions compared to Senna's all-time record of 65. 'No,' Stepney said, 'Ayrton's poles total won't be safe. No, nothing's safe. We've got about another three years of Michael to break the poles and he's not that far behind. In three years he can destroy all that if we can do a good enough job and he can keep his act together. I don't see why he shouldn't.'

However, I still think he's got some things to do which Ayrton just did. I still think Ayrton was the best. Yeah.'

Stepney accepts that they drove in different eras. 'But comparing the two, you have to consider how much help Michael gets with the technology. There was technology years ago, when Ayrton drove, but I'm talking about the *amount*. Michael is not as *manual* as Ayrton: Ayrton did a lot of these things automatically, as did Prost and Lauda and so on, and that is why I still put him that step ahead at the moment. I'm a bit old fashioned about this.'

Stewart, ruminating: 'If you have a racing team, and you're spending all that money on technology – more expensive than ever in the history of motorsport – you'd want the best driver even if you had the very best equipment. The reason is that sometimes a less than great driver can win in the very best car, and it happens – the high technology, traction control, ground effects, everything – but if you look back at the people I'm talking about here, they were never multi-World Champions. They were good enough to win a World Championship if they were in a very good car and a very good team. If somebody's got a very good car they show quite well but you haven't seen them win oodles and oodles of Grands Prix, and you haven't seen them win when everything's gone against them. The difference, I think, is that the great drivers have the capacity to move on from their first championship. It takes an immense amount of commitment, it takes an immense amount of determination, single-mindedness. It's sacrificing all sorts of other things.

The great ones have always been alone in what they could do and how they could do it. Schumacher in Malaysia, 2000.

'At the end of the day there's only six really good drivers on the grid, and out of those six there's maybe only three who are extraordinary but there's always only one genius. Now Schumacher is that genius. I think Häkkinen and Coulthard are the other two in the extraordinary category, while Montoya is up there and Ralf Schumacher is close to being up there.'

The technology became a substitute for skill, and that's why Senna objected to it.

'Yes,' Stewart says, 'but you've still got to look for the fine limit.'

Which explains why, from this theoretical equality, Schumacher has emerged absolutely dominant. He found the fine limit and never forgot where it was.

'He is still able to cream the last little bit out of the milk bar, to take that little bit more out of it than anybody else. What you've got to see is where the cream is lying. Is it in a wee crevasse, is it tucked away where nobody else has noticed it? Will it give me an advantage, be helpful to me? I'll go and look for it and find out where it is and then use the car to take that advantage, which is well hidden from the others. The others are like paper hangers in a thunderstorm [condemned to get wet whatever they do]. They are too busy trying to keep the car on the road to think creatively about where to find an advantage. So it doesn't matter what technology exists: the drivers who are really the best will always take it that little bit further. They won't be flying off the road every five minutes, they won't be one-lap wonders and they won't be one-championship wonders either.'

The matter of difficulty in the cars, then and now, is fascinating.

'Physically you've got power steering, you've got lighter brake pedals, you've got more downforce, more grip, you've got traction control. [At this point in the interview Stewart examined his palms.] 'Still marks there – they bled every race at Monaco and quite a few other racetracks [from gripping the gear knob]. These are just mild differences, however, because we're on a progressive journey from Caracciola[7] and Nuvolari to Fangio and Ascari, then on to Moss and Clark, to Stewart and Fittipaldi, to Prost and Senna. They all had considerably better working environments than the generation before. I had a much cushier job than Caracciola or Nuvolari, I suspect. That's part of evolution, of the adjustment. In order to get the ultimate in performance, man has always – *always* – surpassed whatever technology has been provided. How do you account for the fact that the 4-minute mile is now a slow mile? Man has always extended beyond, and you can't say it is only the latest running shoe. But in motor racing we've now got telemetry, which is objective measurement.'

Does that make Schumacher better than you?

'It doesn't, but it provides the opportunity of using those mechanical devices more productively.'

You or Clark going round Spa had more freedom of choice about what you'd try to make the car do. Now the car is programmed.

'You can still lock up your wheel going in to *Pouhon*, or anywhere else for that matter. Whatever the engineers and the R & D department do, the human remains an amazing animal of chameleon skills. These skills adapt to all the idiosyncrasies which the technologists produce, and they have always adapted. These days they are doing it in extremes which are all different.'

Consider the vintage Ferrari in which Schumacher gave a demonstration run at Silverstone in 2001. In 1951 when it raced and won, it covered 90 laps (418km/260m) at an average speed of 154kmh/96mph. The track measured 4.6km/2.8m and pole was 1:43.400s, an average speed of 161kmh/100mph. Silverstone had no chicanes to slow the cars then and comprised straights linked by five corners and two curves, Chapel and Abbey.

The ten years of Schumacher in Grand Prix racing. The newcomer, 1991. The man with the big future, 1992. The front-runner, 1993. Dressing for a World Championship, 1994 . . .

At the 2001 Grand Prix, the current Ferrari which Schumacher drove covered 60 laps (308kmh/191m) at an average speed of 214kmh/133mph. The track measured 5.1km/3.2m and pole was 1:20.447s, an average speed of 230kmh/142mph. Silverstone had a whole array of features to slow the cars, including a tight horseshoe at Club, a 90 degree left at Abbey and the contorting Bridge-Luffield complex.

In spite of that, Schumacher got round it more than *40mph* faster than the car had done in 1951. These are the extremes which are all different but, as Stewart says, they didn't come from nowhere, they evolved.

To which Stirling Moss says: 'The point is, one learns the tools of one's trade. If you have to cook with a blunt knife, you find different ways of making it cut. It is exactly the same with racing. The technology is a disadvantage for demonstrating a driver's ability: I think that Michael has a greater difficulty now in demonstrating his superiority as blatantly as others in other eras could do. When you start bringing in driver aids, it isn't that the drivers haven't the ability, it's that the best drivers' ability is reduced – or you might say that the lesser drivers' ability is brought up to the common denominator. It negates skill and, expanding on that, I think you'll find that Jacques Villeneuve is against making the circuits too safe: the safer you make them, the greater the contempt of danger you have and, therefore, the drivers' ethics are allowed to lapse.

'The eras change and the style of driving changes and that's why the person who drives today is a glorified go-kart driver – although fantastic in what they do. Fangio would have adapted, I am sure we would, I am sure Jimmy would have done. Of course he would. If that's what you have to do, that's what you do. We had to do things in those days – make allowances because the dampers would get worn and they wouldn't work so well. Things like that don't exist today. When disc brakes came in we learned disc brakes – they were much better than others. But it came in small increments.'

Jo Ramirez has seen every Formula 1 car since 1962 and I wondered if he thought that Clark could have driven Häkkinen's 2001 McLaren, and Häkkinen could have driven Clark's mid-1960s Lotus, without too much difficulty?

'There would be more chance that Clark could have driven Mika's car than the other way round. The cars of today are easier to drive: then they were not easy to drive. The balance of the car was much more critical. They were less forgiving, the tyres were not so good – the tyres were narrow! – and you had to change gears like they don't do now. Changing gear was an art. There were people like Clark and Senna who could change in the middle of a corner to maximise the power of the engine – and everybody says you don't change gear in the corners, you do it before or after. I feel you can learn your trade, and the more you do it the better you get. But at the end of the day nobody is going to teach you how to drive a car better, you have to teach yourself, and from driving it better you can become absolutely superb at it.'

At the Jaguar launch in 2002, Eddie Irvine was questioned about the team principal, Niki Lauda, who intended to drive a modern Formula 1 car hard (he'd done this before, but evidently not *hard*) in order to understand better what the drivers of today were talking about. In the

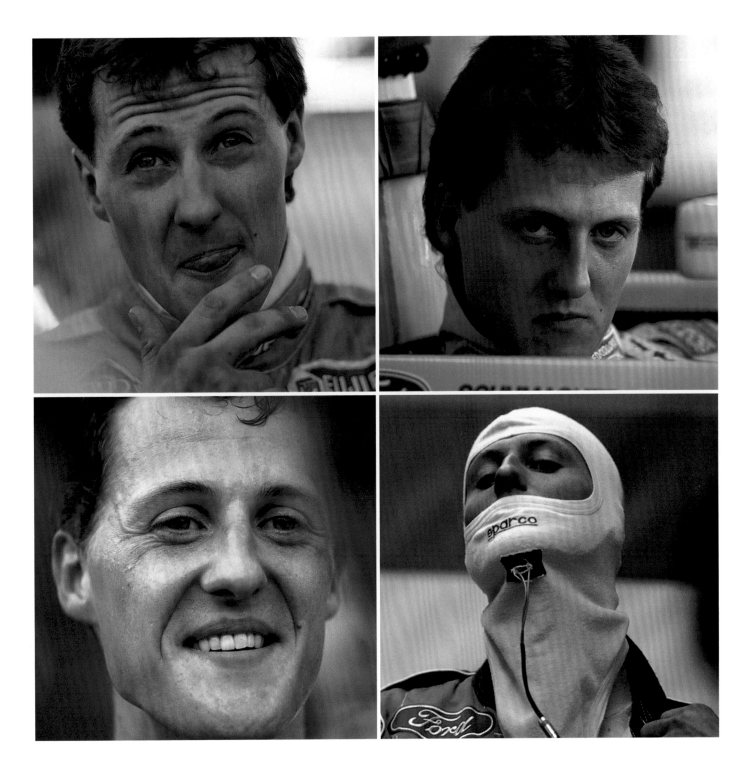

course of his answer Irvine said the cars in Lauda's era were much easier to drive and he knew because he'd driven some. They were like 'saloons'. This runs counter to everything just about anybody has ever said on the subject and, suspecting that Irvine might have said it for just such a reason, I asked him to explain.

'The people who say it was more difficult have probably never done it. The cars were very soft, they weren't as knife-edge to drive, they were very progressive. That's why you could see them going sideways. You watch old film on TV and it's very obvious. They reacted very slowly. Changing gears? You can change gear in your car, can't you? That's the least of your worries. The braking was a lot easier then because they didn't have the stopping power that they have now. You backed off a bit earlier and feathered it through.'

Interesting, as they say.

The modern racing driver, particularly if he achieves the status and global recognition of Schumacher, risks being overwhelmed – mobbed – unless he controls his life very carefully. Essentially this means living in a sort of seclusion. Evidently even Monte Carlo became too much for Schumacher and he has retreated to his home in Switzerland from within which he is able to live a family life.

Showing them how it's done, Argentina, 1995.

Ramirez ruminates that the modern successful drivers 'cannot appreciate their own wealth because they've always had it. They say Schumacher was very upset about what happened on 11 September [the terrorist attacks in the United States]. I'm sure he was. Maybe it was because he'd never experienced the real world, whereas Ayrton had been exposed to it in Brazil even though he came from a wealthy family. In fact Ayrton was more exposed to life and he had to work for it a little harder than Schumacher.'

Jackie Stewart, speaking in 2002, remarked on how closed Schumacher's world seemed to be and that he didn't show much interest in anything beyond it. I agreed and assume just about everybody else would too. In one very important sense, we were all wrong. Schumacher had been moving beyond his world for ten years – but quietly. This is described in **Facts of the matter** at the end of the chapter but first, here is what Stewart said:

'You could say Schumacher's got all the money he needs, he's got a family, he's got everything else and driving a Grand Prix car is safer than fishing, or rugby, or boxing, or mountaineering.

'Does he want to continue to drive himself and only be interested in a single-minded way? I think he is limited to one area of performance and I don't think he has great ambitions to say "oh, I really would love to do this" about something else. For example he goes up to Norway for the winter and gets away from everybody else, so he doesn't want to go to dinner parties, he doesn't want to go to cocktail parties, he doesn't want to meet anybody else that's famous: no ambitions in that respect. He doesn't want to build a skyscraper. Ayrton was beginning to be quite interested in business, interested in things beyond the pit and paddock.

'I don't think Schumacher's got a lot of curiosity, and that's the thing which attracts most people to look at other things. You're curious. *What does it take to do this*, or *why would you do that?* It's nothing to do with money. When I did that movie with Roman Polanski[8] I thought: Roman Polanski's so clever and such a creator that it would be really nice to work with somebody like him. It gave me another dimension.'

You have mastered the art of public speaking.

'I'm sure Michael isn't interested in doing that, because if he was he'd have done it. If he'd like to speak at the United Nations he could. I spoke to 8,000 people recently and to do that you've got to be pretty sure you've got your priorities together – it's live, it's not recorded. You've got to do it right, and to do that you've got to have a desire to do it. I'm not sure Michael has reached that point – but it may come.

'I'm talking about beyond doing expert commentaries on the races on TV – that would be the easy option, as James Hunt did and Martin Brundle is doing, but Martin does other things, TV programmes which aren't about racing. And he has a business, and he's with the BRDC.[9] That's because you're curious, you want to try and do other things. I don't think Michael is interested in looking at other people's views in a way that would allow him to be exposed to them, even in a peripheral way. For me, he should be improving himself. You could say that he doesn't need self-improvement but I think everybody needs it.'

He's got his place in Switzerland and he only seems to need to move around within the Grand Prix world or go to far away places to get fit in the winter.

'That's where I think he is missing such a lot, with the entrée that he has. In that sense he could be very big and multi-coloured, a kaleidoscope if he wanted, but at the moment it's very mono-colour. It's bright red. When I met Polanski I was interested in listening to Polanski. When I met the King of Jordan I just wanted to be exposed to the King or Jordan as much as I could. You don't prostitute yourself for that – because he wanted to meet me, in the same way that somebody would want to meet Michael. Having met them you develop within yourself. My hope is that Michael will develop from where he is, because not every sportsman does that. It's a rarity, but it is also important, because when you're a sportsman you're so spoiled.'

Now, maybe, we can reach towards a conclusion, which of course is not the same thing as the answer to The Biggest Question.

We've examined the cars of different eras, and compared the driving of them. We haven't considered how strong the competition was, and Gary Anderson offers cautionary words about that in a general reflection. 'With a lot of sports you have easier opportunities than motor racing. How many people are out there playing golf at different levels before you get to the top? And think how much cheaper it is to do, because you only need a set of golf clubs. In tennis it's a racket, in soccer a football and so on. You don't need £10,000s in equipment

before you can compete – and, incidentally, the more equipment you need, the greater the risk of some of it being bad! The guys who get to the top in motor racing aren't necessarily the good guys. The odd one does – like Michael.'

Even keeping these words in mind, Fangio had to compete against Moss (and vice versa, of course) but also Ascari, the ferocious Giuseppe Farina, Mike Hawthorn and Peter Collins. Clark had Graham Hill, John Surtees, Jack Brabham and Stewart.

Now listen to Jo Ramirez. 'I spoke to Alain before Senna came to McLaren [in 1988] and he said "I'll have anybody". Schumacher won the championship two years against Damon Hill, two years against Mika Häkkinen – well, one year against David Coulthard. I'm not taking anything away from those guys, but I am saying they were the only ones Schumacher had to race against. Senna raced against Prost, against Mansell, against Piquet, against Rosberg, all of those people who were top guys. They were winning Grands Prix and championships.'

Stewart insists that 'there's nobody as close to Schumacher' – in terms of ability – 'as there was to Senna' and Moss reinforces that. 'The thing that Michael has at the moment is the biggest gap between himself and the next guy, the number 2 to him if you like. It may be closing, it may not, but if you go back six months or a year the guy you consider number 2 – Mika or David or whoever – was nowhere near Michael's ability, and that's the gap.'

Jody Scheckter reinforces *that*. 'It could be said that he is the best driver of all times. However, Ayrton Senna was racing against Alain Prost and vice versa, and they could both be contenders for the best. Michael is not up against that level of competition. That is the only argument against him being the best of all time.'

Gary Anderson invokes Prost and Senna, but in a different way. 'I think you have to consider Michael among the greatest drivers since 1950 and I don't think we've seen the end of it yet. I'm putting Michael in front of Ayrton. He's more complete. If you took Senna and Prost – Senna was the ultimate go-out-and-do-the-job, pick it up and throw it round, and Prost was The Professor. Michael is a combination of both of them.'

Jean-Louis Schlesser who was at Mercedes in sports cars at the same time as Schumacher – and nearly got on the wrong end of Derek Warwick's wrath when Schumacher ought to have been the recipient – has been watching motorsport these many years as well as competing. 'If you want to compare Schumacher with somebody, and it's very hard, there is one guy. Fangio. For me he was something absolutely special because he won five titles with different cars. You remember when the Maserati was a piece of rubbish, nobody wanted it, and he made the car into a winner. Jim Clark also was something exceptional. I was very young when I saw him but he impressed me a lot. You can put Schumacher at the top, you can put Schumacher with Fangio.'

Belgium 2001, proving that the shortest route between two points is over the kerbs. In the race Schumacher stroked the Ferrari home ahead of David Coulthard in the McLaren.

The implication is that Schumacher joins Fangio, not supplants him.

Stirling Moss does not agree. 'He is an exceptional driver and in the top six of all time but he has nowhere near the ability of Fangio. In my mind Fangio was the greatest driver. I don't even know if Michael's reached the ability of Senna, I don't know if he's reached the ability of Clark.' Moss, speaking to me in 2002, accepted that Schumacher could beat Fangio's total of five and Senna's 65 poles.

Stewart agreed. 'There are 17 races a year, 16 minimum. If Ferrari are able to keep the edge, and Schumacher keeps his, it's very possible – because he's being very focused and very aggressive and demanding and unyielding. That's what keeps a team like Ferrari on that edge and that's where it is possible.' This does not lure Stewart into answering The Question, however. Instead he repeats: 'All you can do is give the ones who dominated in their eras. Who were the absolute leaders during that period? Who were the dominant individuals?'

In every sport which can be measured, *everything* has improved to a degree which is almost embarrassing in any comparison between then and now. I've covered Roger Bannister's mile in a footnote so here's another example, this one chosen at random. In 1928 the great Finnish runner Parvo Nurmi won the 10,000 metre Olympic title with a time of 30m 18.8secs. The current world record, held by Haile Gebrselassie, stands at 26m 22.75secs – nearly four minutes faster. He'd have beaten Nurmi by more than three laps of the track. And so it goes, everywhere you look.

Why should this – mysteriously and suspiciously – not apply to those sports which cannot be measured, the football, the cricket, the tennis and the golf? And where does that leave the racing driver, always a prisoner of the car he has to drive? The world of Nurmi was simplicity itself. He ran. The world of Fangio was complicated by what he could make the car do, and that's the same for Schumacher. In that sense, the faster lap times argue for the impact of technology rather than a parallel increase in driving skill.

I think the crucial difference is that Fangio had scope to be a genius because the circumstances – cars, rules, circuits, attitudes, demands – were looser. Schumacher has conjured beautiful, magical races out of tightness: car construction controlled, a thick book of rules, electronic aids equalising ability, circuits neutered for safety, attitudes born of business, plus voracious demands on every aspect of him every moment.

Perhaps that is a clue.

Fangio was the undisputed master before technology became dominant, Schumacher is the undisputed master after it became dominant, so that, between them, they cover the two most distinctive eras. Moss, Clark and Senna fall quite naturally into the evolution between. If you accept this, you are left with just the two, Fangio and Schumacher. Which?

Nobody knows that.

NOTES

[1] Among the few racers he encountered, Moss places Jean Behra, the Frenchman who drove in 52 Grands Prix before being killed at the Avus circuit, Berlin, in 1959.

[2] Bahamas Speed Week, in fact known as the Nassau Speed Week. In 1959, en route to the US Grand Prix at Sebring, Florida, Jack Brabham went to it and wrote (in *When the Flag Drops*, William Kimber, 1971) 'I rested on the Saturday in preparation for the International Nassau Trophy, the main event on the Sunday. The race was originally scheduled for 56 laps (250 miles) but eventually it was curtailed to 49 laps and ended at 5.30pm because of bad light. Sixty-five drivers took part: they included Moss.' The cars included Porsches, Aston Martins and Ferraris.

[3] Fangio's native language was Spanish and in those days English had not yet become a necessity for anyone within motorsport.

[4] In this chapter I have confined myself to drivers of the World Championship, which began in 1950.

By definition that excludes all the pre-War drivers, and so we don't have Tazio Nuvolari who was great by any definition. He was a racer and regularly drove cars to destruction rather than finish second.

[5] Roger Bannister (now Sir) ran the first 4-minute mile at Oxford in 1954. He did 3m 59.4 and was so exhausted he virtually collapsed. The current record [in January 2002] is held by the Moroccan Hicham El Guerrouj who, at Rome in 1999, did 3m 43.13. The difference in the two times – slightly over 16 seconds – is difficult to even imagine.

[6] Chris Amon, a popular New Zealander, drove 96 Grands Prix between 1963 and 1976 – changing teams frequently – but never won a race.

[7] Rudi Caracciola (1901–1959) was a highly talented German driver of the 1930s.

[8] Roman Polanski, the Polish film director of such films as *Repulsion* (with Catherine Deneuve) and *Rosemary's Baby* (with Mia Farrow) made a documentary about Stewart's weekend at the Monaco Grand Prix in the early 1970s.

[9] British Racing Drivers' Club, based at Silverstone.

Facts of the matter

The broadening of Michael Schumacher began in the most unexpected way. Let him tell in his own words, spoken in 2002, how he first had the idea of helping children.

'It was long before I took up Formula 1 racing. When I was driving in Formula Three, I was in a couple of races, in Macau and Fuji. The winner of both would scoop $30,000. I got lucky. Nobody could believe it. It was then I realised I could help people. I'd never had money before. From the time I started earning more money than I ever dreamt of, I felt the need to help children. You either feel that or you don't at such times.'

How did you come into contact with UNESCO[1] and why did you decide to work with it?

Rubens Barrichello and Jean Todt help Schumacher celebrate his fourth World Championship, in Hungary, 2001. Wet faces, big smile.

'I'd been looking for a way to help people since 1990. The contact came through Mrs Ute-Henriette Ohoven, UNESCO's Goodwill Ambassador for the Education of "Children in Need". The idea was to take part in a UNESCO project, to work together. I was delighted, and especially by the general idea of UNESCO – of creating conditions to give people a future and help them to be self sufficient.'

You donated 1.5 million Euros for projects in Senegal, Sarajevo and Peru. Why these countries?

'UNESCO presented me with these situations that it knew well. The projects looked good.'

Have you donated money to other institutions that help children?

'I give a bit here and there for small projects, but the main ones are those that have developed with UNESCO. I think it's good to be consistent.'

Does consistency inspire confidence?

'Yes, of course. First of all I feel it in myself and then in others who commit themselves to projects because I'm involved in them. I can't pay for everything. I sign up for various efforts for a while and this attracts other donors to help out. People are encouraged to give when they know it goes to UNESCO projects. They're confident the money will be used well.'

Have you visited the projects you've funded – the school in Senegal, the clinic in Sarajevo and the centre for street children in Peru?

'I've been to Sarajevo, but not yet to Senegal and Peru, where the project has only just started. I have a hectic life, so it's not always easy to fit everything in.'

Do you have a favourite kind of project?

'I really want to help the ones people don't know about. Nowadays, certain projects attract lots of donors. Then there are others you never hear about. Those are the ones I'm interested in.'

One of the reasons Jackie Stewart and most other people didn't know about this was that Schumacher did it all discreetly. The UNESCO staff who've met him are impressed by this, as they are by the man himself. They find him entirely normal, almost shy and good company.

He was made a UNESCO Champion for Sport in April 2002, 'in recognition of his role in the promotion of sport, his contribution to UNESCO's educational action in favour of young people all over the world, and his dedication to the Organisation's ideals.'

That happened at UNESCO's Paris headquarters and they filled out the background to what he had been doing, pointing out that he had 'donated 250,000 Deutschmarks to UNESCO, money paid to him by the German magazine *Bunte* for exclusive photos of his wedding. Further substantial donations by him enabled the building of a school in Dakar (Senegal) in 1996 and improvements to be made in the city's slum suburb of Baraka as part of a joint UNESCO/Enda Third World [2] project.

'In 1997, his generosity made possible the opening in Sarajevo of a clinic to help child war victims heal their psychological wounds and teach young amputees to use artificial limbs. Schumacher's donations will fund the opening, in Lima (Peru), of a "Palace of the Poor", a centre

for street children that will provide them with shelter, food, medical care and pre-school education.'

Schumacher is also a special ambassador to the Principality of San Marino (and so is Jean Todt). The San Marino Grand Prix, of course, is run at Imola in Italy but that doesn't matter.

On the Thursday before the US Grand Prix in 2003, Schumacher and Todt went in their official capacity to visit the Riley Hospital for Children in Indianapolis. This was, incidentally, Schumacher's debut as an ambassador. The hospital, one of the most advanced in America, looks after more than 200,000 patients a year.

He and Todt were met by Professor Howard Eigen, director of the Lung and Intensive Care department and

went to the infant tumour department, where they chatted with the children and handed over a model of the Ferrari F2002.

Professor Eigen said: 'We are really grateful to Jean Todt and Michael Schumacher. The children and their families and also all of us have really appreciated their generosity and the feeling of warmth which it generated. The smiles on the faces of our little patients is its most eloquent proof.'

[1] United Nations Educational, Scientific and Cultural Organisation.
[2] Enda Tiers Monde (Third World), an international non-profit making organisation based in Senegal, which is tackling poverty and encouraging both human rights and development.

Chapter Eleven

CROWN JEWELS

On the last day of the 2000 season, Michael Schumacher could reflect that Ferrari now had a World Champion again and he had his third title: he had become the sixth driver in history to achieve three. Ahead lay Prost on four and Fangio on five, of course. If we were not in it before, we were in it now: the Schumacher era. That, as we've seen through the book, involved a consistency of F1 domination never met before, and however much it was a product of rigorous (and sometimes inspired) teamwork, Schumacher was the one who delivered.

The Schumacher era existed at two levels. Mentally it was a tour de force by one man and his multi-national company, and physically a massacre. Across 2001 and 2002, as he set himself up for the season attacking Fangio's summit in 2003, he won *twenty* of the 34 Grands prix, took *eighteen* poles and amassed 267 points (Barrichello next, 133). This, as we have seen, threatened the wellbeing of Formula 1 itself because the millions of tele-viewers who had just a mild interest in the sport simply turned off: there seemed no point in watching. Some behaved tactically, watching the start and the finish only. Many stopped altogether.

To the connoisseur, however, Schumacher was now operating at a level where the expression of his art – its purity, its certainty, its intellectual ability to mould movement – was more like a necklace of polished gems than a sequence of races.

2001

A race and a championship were compressed into a few seconds one August afternoon and, when it was done, Michael Schumacher found this compression of words to describe it: 'A beautiful weekend'.

Grandstand view of Schumacher's fourth win in 2002, Barcelona.

In those first few seconds he thrust his Ferrari from pole position to the first corner of the Hungaroring. This was more than taking the lead in the Hungarian Grand Prix, it was the decisive moment of the race and it would bring the World Championship with it. For the next hour and 41 minutes Schumacher circled essentially alone, at his own pace and in his own time. This was a master at the height of his art, smoothing the ferocity of a racing car into a great simplicity, soothing the turbulence of a Grand Prix into a processional thing, and utterly under his control. The French sports daily *L'Equipe* compressed that into a headline across their front page next day:

SCHUMI ALONE IN THE WORLD

He was.

You cannot pretend that the Hungarian Grand Prix was a gripping race in any meaningful sense because Schumacher and Ferrari were now too good to permit anything like that.

They came to the Hungaroring, the thirteenth of the 17 rounds, with Schumacher on 84 points and David Coulthard (McLaren) on 47, a differential so enormous that the championship was not gripping either. Schumacher was going to win it somewhere, sometime. Here? Ferrari's Technical Director Ross Brawn – most shrewd reader of men, machines and moments – surveyed Schumacher and judged him to be in 'great shape'. The championship pressure, Brawn concluded, has been passed from him to the other drivers who had to try to catch him.

Schumacher confirmed how relaxed he felt but said this 'wasn't a tactic to stop putting too much pressure on myself. It was just like that, not deliberate at all.' He even told Jean Todt, the Ferrari team boss, 'you know, I haven't got a very good feeling, I'm not sure that this is the weekend we'll do it'.

He chanced to meet Alain Prost, then running his own team, the day before the race and Prost told him to win. Prost had held the record number of victories, 51, since 1993 and was bored having to talk endlessly about it. Schumacher, having to talk endlessly about beating it, replied 'I feel exactly the same'. Schumacher had 50. This was really what the Hungaroring was about: not just a World Championship but helping to establish Schumacher's place in history. He had been in Grand Prix racing for a decade and now, in his maturity, all manner of records were tumbling towards him. Records may or may not be an accurate gauge of a driver, although if he has won more races than anybody else, taken more points and put himself within one of equalling the most championships it must tell us something.

Jo Ramirez, McLaren's team co-ordinator and a man fiercely proud of the team, points out that 'Alain had, I think, 30 wins when he was with us.' Out of loyalty to what Prost had achieved at McLaren, Ramirez told him 'Michael is very close to breaking your record and we are going to do everything in our power to stop him doing it this year.'

Whatever his feelings about whether or not the championship would be won in Hungary, Schumacher established a mood by going fastest on the Friday, Coulthard tenth. Coulthard 'hit the kerb at an unfortunate angle, damaging the chassis,' in the first of the two sessions and couldn't drive in the second.

On the Saturday Schumacher required only two runs. Moving towards the half hour, Häkkinen had provisional pole with 1m 15.41. Schumacher forced that to 1m 14.41 and it stayed there until, with 20 minutes to go, he forced it to 1m 14.05. This was itself a compression of a lap, to which he brought so much balance and so much speed that, as someone observed, it appeared to defy physics. Coulthard produced a forceful lap to join him on the front row but 0.801 seconds slower. This is what such a gap represented, set against the preceding five years:

1996 (Schumacher from Hill)	0.05
1997 (Schumacher from Villeneuve)	0.1
1998 (Häkkinen from Coulthard)	0.1
1999 (Häkkinen from Coulthard)	0.1
2000 (Schumacher from Coulthard)	0.3
Now…	
2001 (Schumacher from Coulthard)	0.8

Schumacher stayed true to his philosophy of pragmatism although he did allow himself a superlative or two. Psychology? It certainly can't have helped Coulthard. 'I am surprised at this lap time because it is much quicker than our predictions suggested. It's the result of a perfect lap and a car that was already 100% in the morning. I only did six laps' – out lap, fast lap, in lap, twice – 'but not to save tyres.

I just felt I had got the maximum out of myself and the car so it was better to sit rather than waste effort.'

Brawn said: 'An exceptional performance from Michael. The fact that he won the championship last year has made this season less stressful for him. I have seen no signs of pressure.'

He'd had the car through a gravel trap on the warm-up lap – at Turn 12, the right-hander before the left-loop and the pits – and that stirred a flurry of activity from the mechanics when he'd settled it on the bay for pole.

He led the parade lap knowing that, historically, he who reaches Turn 1 in the lead can then command the race. At the instant the five red lights blinked off Schumacher was away, Barrichello working a path in behind him and going over to the right, masking Turn 1 from Coulthard. Schumacher, ahead, was away free.

And that was the completion of the compression.

Barrichello would ride shotgun behind, masking Coulthard from the whole maddening point-and-squirt circuit. Completing the opening lap Schumacher had siphoned out a lead of 1.3 seconds, next lap it was 1.3, the lap after that 1.3, then 1.2, then 1.4. On lap 7 it was 1.3, and Coulthard was hammering out fastest lap after fastest lap but still Barrichello stayed ahead of him. And on lap 9 Barrichello cut the gap to Schumacher to 0.9 seconds.

Jean Todt carried the weight and never let it show. Suzuka, 2000, the championship finally won and no emotion left unturned.

The received wisdom – born, nurtured and confirmed during Schumacher's decade of Grand Prix racing – was that if you gave him the lead you didn't see him again, never mind cut gaps. Here at the Hungaroring he was happy to go round and round preserving his tyres, as he would say, 'for later'. Later he simply accelerated. The fractions are important to underscore how it happened. On lap 11 he set fastest lap and made the lead 2.7 (Coulthard @ 3.4), on lap 12 it was 3.4 – fastest lap again – and out it went, to 4.1, 4.4, 5.3 (fastest lap). On lap 16 he broke Nigel Mansell's record set in 1992. By the posture of the Ferrari on the track you would never have known Schumacher had just done such a thing, because this was the control of a master: to settle himself and the car down and, when he was ready – while never looking faster – to increase his pace to the point where nobody else could stay with him. It is one of those things the very greatest can do: go fast slowly whenever they wish, as their fellow drivers run breathless trying to keep near.

The rest passed into history, Schumacher pitting and regaining the lead, repeating this at the second pit stops then cantering it. He'd say that 'later in the race' Barrichello 'gave me a lot of pressure'. He'd add that 'towards the end I was worried about making a mistake because one car was leaving oil on the track'. He needn't have worried. He did not permit himself to think he would take the championship until three laps from the end when he thought 'now this has the feeling of it being here, truly!' He won it by some four seconds and, on the slowing down lap, couldn't find the words to radio to the team so he said it was 'amazing. It is so lovely to work with you guys.'

Coulthard finished third.

'I might be a good driver but I am not good at finding the right words to describe this,' Schumacher would say. He paid due tribute to the team. 'They are wonderful guys and we have stuck together through the good and the bad times and I am really in love with all of them.'

This was his fourth championship, drawing level with Prost, so that only Juan-Manuel Fangio's five remained to beat. Out of interest, this is the group on three championships which Schumacher had now left: Sir Jack Brabham, Sir Jackie Stewart, Niki Lauda, Nelson Piquet and Ayrton Senna.

Only one man had ever won back-to-back championships with Ferrari: Alberto Ascari in 1952/53. Several factors had helped him, apart from the fact that he was a superb driver. The Ferrari proved to be the dominant car in both seasons and his rival Fangio was absent in 1952. Ascari, moreover, was competing against small fields and many of the drivers were known for competence rather than conquest. Arguably, Schumacher had it tougher, against Häkkinen and Coulthard at McLaren, and brother Ralf and Juan-Pablo Montoya at resurgent Williams.

Moving into the 2001 season, records had been coming steadily into view. You can feel ambivalent about the relevance of statistics and how accurate they are as a gauge, but when many of the major all-time records are at one man's mercy you cannot ignore them.

Beginning 2001, this was the situation.

Prost had most points (798.5), Schumacher next (678). With 17 races in 2001, Prost's total was potentially vulnerable.

Senna had most poles (65), Clark and Prost 33, Schumacher and Nigel Mansell 32. Senna's total would be out of reach for at least three seasons.

Prost had most wins (51), Schumacher 44, Senna 41. Prost's total was vulnerable.

Prost and Schumacher shared the number of fastest laps (41) from Mansell, 30. That would go very quickly, probably at the first race.

Schumacher was in good spirits. 'I feel well. I had a good rest and I am in top form.' The new car, the F-2001, was launched at the Fiorano circuit on 29 January, Schumacher making all the right noises. Villeneuve and Schumacher had had a sharp relationship for years and round about now Villeneuve said he had qualms about racing Schumacher because 'you don't know if the track will be wide enough, you don't know if he has seen you and it is very difficult to judge, whereas with Mika [Häkkinen], he thinks like a normal human being.'

It is true that Schumacher often adopted robust tactics at the start of a race, ruthlessly protecting his lead from the lights to the first corner. But apart from that, what Villeneuve implied seemed largely to have disappeared: the crashes with Damon Hill, Villeneuve and even David Coulthard, and the anger they had brought, were years ago. In Formula 1 terms, Schumacher was now into comfortable middle age and supervising the kids rather than barging and bumping a path through them.

He drove the new car at Fiorano on 1 February, and rather solemnly Ferrari pointed out that it 'carried the Number 1 for the first time'. No Ferrari had done that since 1980. 'The first impression is very good. The car is very competitive.' He hadn't slept well before the test. 'I was a little bit nervous', but he wasn't nervous after it.

The first race – Melbourne in 2001 – is invariably an accurate guide to the rest of the season. The fast cars are

already fast, the slower cars will have enormous difficulty making up the difference.

Schumacher crashed heavily on the Friday. Under yellow flags 'I was really on the limit. I touched the brakes a little bit harder to slow down enough for the situation and that's why I lost the back end. It was not actually a heavy impact because I did not hit the wall, so it was just a gentle roll and I am fine.'

Next day he put the F-2001 on pole, from Barrichello, and led throughout the race except for the pit stops. Schumacher had now matured to the point where he could pace himself as if the others weren't there, drive comparatively slowly when he wished and still win.

During the race a marshal was killed when a wheel from Villeneuve's car struck him. Schumacher, shocked like everybody else, said 'we must see what can be done to improve their working conditions from a safety point of view.' People previously convinced that Schumacher was a cold and calculating man had somehow to reconcile this

with the way he betrayed the most human emotions – including tears at the death of a marshal at Monza the previous season – and invariably found the right words to cover the sombre moments.

He took pole in Malaysia and made a powerful start to the race, Barrichello behind him, but on the third lap rain fell and both Ferraris skated off like synchronised swimmers. They resumed with Barrichello third, Schumacher seventh and the rain became a tempest. Cars were going off everywhere and the Safety Car came out.

The Ferraris pitted on lap 4 but by now the confusion of the race had reached into the team. Brawn saw Barrichello skate off a second time and assumed, incorrectly, that Schumacher was now in front of him again. The mechanics assumed Schumacher would be pitting first and were ready for him – then Barrichello arrived. In this confusion they fitted Schumacher's tyres to Barrichello's car and had to take them off again. Barrichello was stationary for 72 seconds, Schumacher patiently waiting his turn parked

behind him. Schumacher's pit stop took 8.0 seconds but, cumulatively, lasted 80 seconds plus the time it had taken him to slow and would now take getting back to the track.

It is at such moments that Schumacher presents his willpower, his breadth of vision and his ability to apply genius to racecraft. Where so many drivers would accept that the race had gone from them, he saw only advantages to be exploited. He had intermediate tyres on and the circuit was a monsoon on one side, dry on the other. That was one method of exploitation, sailing safely through the monsoon, accelerating into the dry.

The Safety Car circled so that he and Barrichello would catch up the snake of cars following it and, when the re-start came, they would have regained most of the time lost in the pits. It was something else to be exploited, and no matter that, as Schumacher joined the tail of the snake, 'the conditions were atrocious and undrivable, and at times the Safety Car was quicker than us'.

At the re-start, on lap 11, Barrichello ran tenth and

Schumacher eleventh. Completing that lap Barrichello was up to eighth, Schumacher ninth, @ 10.06 seconds from the leader, Coulthard. In the rolling spray the sleek-nosed Ferraris were moving like a pair of sharks. Schumacher overtook Barrichello and they hunted down Jarno Trulli in the Jordan: Schumacher sixth, @ 8.91 from Coulthard. They hunted down Frentzen in the other Jordan, Schumacher describing a great arc of power outside him. Schumacher drew up to Ralf and dealt with him almost immediately. And, describing another great arc, went outside Häkkinen. On lap 13 Schumacher was third, @ 6.27 from Coulthard. He caught Jos Verstappen (Arrows) and pressured him, placed the Ferrari inside as they approached a right-hander, and he was second.

Coulthard was within reach and for once Schumacher pushed so hard that the Ferrari shivered. The gap to Coulthard was down to 1.96. He tried the arc of power but Coulthard resisted. On the start-finish straight he squeezed up behind Coulthard, came out and went round the outside. The race was decided and the records were falling to him. This was

Schumacher's sixth Grand Prix victory in succession, taking him past the five of Brabham (1960), Jim Clark (1965) and Mansell (1992). Ahead lay Ascari with nine (1952–53).

He didn't reach that – second in Brazil to Coulthard – and he retired at Imola with a mechanical problem. That did not prevent him expressing delight that Ralf won. 'This is the first time that two brothers have won Formula 1 Grands Prix.'

He won Spain, although that was inherited because Häkkinen broke down at the end, and was second in Austria (to Coulthard) despite a brush with Montoya. 'The fight had been fair until the incident,' Schumacher said. 'Then he tried to take me out at the corner and I had to go onto the grass because I could not turn in. He was not looking where he was going, he was looking where I was going.'

On 22 May, Ferrari announced that Schumacher and Barrichello had extended their contracts, Schumacher to the end of 2004 and Barrichello to the end of 2002.

Monaco? Let Schumacher describe it. 'In some ways it was an easy and straightforward race because I was out in front on my own but at the same time it was quite hard as we still had to do fast lap times. The traction control made the race rougher physically as we are going quicker. I love the circuit – it is always a challenge. Today I just had to think about reliability and make sure I didn't make a mistake. I asked Ross Brawn what some other drivers were doing and he told me to concentrate. I had no problem with back-markers and my car was pretty good, even if I did not push 100% because in the early stages when Mika was behind me I was trying to look after the car and the tyres.'

This was the seventh race and made the championship points Schumacher 52, Coulthard 40. Schumacher now put a strong run together which virtually settled the title: second in Canada to Ralf – who beat him in a straight fight – then winning the European at the Nürburgring after squeezing Ralf very, very hard at the start. The pit lane wall was not far away. 'The start was a kind of key to the race and I had to do anything I could to keep Ralf behind me. I left him room and it was hard, I know that, but it was necessary for me because I knew I was on two stops and I didn't know what Ralf was on.' After the race Ralf was so enraged he did not trust himself to speak.

Schumacher won in France and was second in Britain (to Häkkinen) so that he had 84 points, Coulthard 47. The championship had become when, not if – although not at Hockenheim where he had a gear selection problem from the grid and Luciano Burti (Prost) helplessly ran into the back of him. Since Coulthard didn't finish – a mechanical problem – the points remained the same. Schumacher travelled to the Hungaroring nursing the conviction that the championship wouldn't be settled there. As we have seen, his conviction was misplaced.

There remained Belgium, Italy, the USA and Japan.

At Spa he qualified third and won a bizarre race when both Williamses ahead of him had problems at the start and re-start, but the next two races were pitched into shadows and personal questioning. The terrorist attack on the twin towers in New York was on 11 September, Monza on 16 September. Schumacher felt in no mood to celebrate the World Championship. He questioned aloud the wisdom of going to the United States Grand Prix – Indianapolis was on 30 September – and, just before the race at *Budapest.* Monza, tried to persuade the drivers to go in grid *The amphitheatre* order through the first two chicanes after the red *moved.* lights as a safety precaution. He finished the race fourth and went quietly away. Evidently he had even considered retirement from F1.

They all did go to Indianapolis and he finished second. It scarcely seemed to interest him and mentally he was somewhere else. That didn't apply to Suzuka in mid-October where he lifted the willpower and racecraft to a new level in qualifying. He made three runs for grid position and each of them would have been ample for pole. The Suzuka circuit is a glorious examination of car and driver, and demands imagination to master it. Schumacher's third run – which of course he had no need to make and appeared as a gesture of personal satisfaction – became a mesmeric thing. He danced the Ferrari through Suzuka's 18 curves, corners and chicane, danced it for 3.6 miles. This wasn't rock 'n' roll, wasn't disco, it had the elegance of a ballroom quickstep, each precise movement flowing into the next. He did 1m 32.48 and it was, as someone murmured in awe, the perfect lap. Montoya was next with 1m 33.18.

Breathless, the team announced: 'Eleventh pole position of the season for Ferrari and Michael Schumacher, a season record for both the team and driver. This is Michael's 43rd career pole, his sixth at Suzuka. It is the team's 148th pole, the fifth at this event.' In Ferrari terms, the eleven beat the nine of Schumacher in 2000, and Lauda in 1974 and 1975. The eleven was still short of Mansell (14, 1992, Williams), Senna (13, 1988 and 1989, McLaren), Prost (13, 1993, Williams). It equalled Häkkinen's 11 in 1999 (McLaren).

At the start of the race he moved diagonally across, blocking Montoya – a favoured tactic but somehow brutal in its intent – and guarded the racing line through Turn One. Schumacher shed Montoya and … well, you know the story. You've heard it a time or two before.

He had now scored more Grand Prix points – 801 – than Prost's 798.5. He had 123 points in the season, beating the record of 108 he held with Nigel Mansell (Schumacher achieved this in 2000, Mansell in 1992). It was 'the perfect

end to the season'. After the race he looked as he habitually did: fresh, at ease.

Rory Byrne designed the F-2001. By nature he is a quiet man and rarely goes to the races. Like many genuine artists (and a Formula 1 designer is certainly that) he prefers to let what he creates speak for itself. This, however, is his summary of the 2001 season, exquisite in its brevity.

'Michael was under real pressure when he came second in the championship in 1997, second in 1998 and then had the crash at Silverstone in 1999. It meant that the pressure went onto 2000. Since then, when that particular pressure came off, he's been driving even better. The 2001 championship wasn't as easy as it might have looked. What helped us was our reliability, which the opposition lacked. They could perhaps match us for speed but not reliability. I think what has happened at Ferrari is important for Formula 1. I was in South Africa recently [at the end of the 2001 season] and the interest and enthusiasm was genuinely unbelievable. That's when you realise.'

2002

On the evening of 21 July 2002, Formula 1's greatest strength had become, as already said, potentially a lethal weakness. That strength – the cumulative accomplishments of the whole Ferrari team, brought to an astonishing pitch by Michael Schumacher – had just won the French Grand Prix and the World Championship, and equalled Fangio's five titles.

Before we get into the cut and thrust of 2002, here are the number of rounds that drivers have taken to win the title in recent years:

1990 and 1991	Senna	15/16
1992	Mansell	11/16
1993	Prost	14/16
1994	Schumacher	16/16
1995	Schumacher	15/17
1996	Hill	16/16
1997	Villeneuve	17/17
1998 and 1999	Häkkinen	16/16
2000	Schumacher	16/17
2001	Schumacher	13/17
2002	Schumacher	11/17

The 2002 title was settled with six races and three months to spare. In sum, from Australia at the beginning of March he'd put this together: victory, third and pole, victory, victory and pole, victory and pole, victory, second, victory, second, victory, victory.

It's easy for your eyes to glaze over by such a list, so consider three aspects.

Of the eleven races to France, he'd won all but three and his lowest place was *third* in Malaysia where, after a crash with Montoya on the opening lap, he had been *twenty-third*.

From the eleven races he had only three poles. In Austria, Monaco, the Nürburgring and Silverstone he hadn't even been on the front row. He and the Ferrari F2002 had reached the point where they were massacring even the importance of grid positions.

Of the eleven, he had set only three fastest laps. Perhaps he'd have had more if he'd cared to but was following Jackie Stewart's dictum that you win the races as slowly as possible. He'd finish the season with a career total of 51 (from Prost 41, Mansell 30, Clark 28) but, on the way to France in 2002, he was taking the championship with such overwhelming superiority that fastest laps were no more than optional exclamation marks.

The season began quietly enough, with Luca Badoer and Luciano Burti, the test drivers, lapping Barcelona on 8 January. Schumacher first drove at Fiorano on 14 January. The traditional build-up had begun. Schumacher first drove the new car, the F2002, at Fiorano in early February and said it was 'very promising'.

Urgent and controversial consultations before the 2001 Italian Grand Prix, Schumacher pleading for the drivers to take it easy through the first chicane.

The Ferrari F2001 – cloaked in mystery.

The crushing win, San Marino.

The team took the old car to Melbourne, however, for the first race and on the first day Schumacher and Barrichello were the only ones in the 1.27s. This prompted Brawn to say 'of course the other teams are running new cars which might have more potential than ours, but I think we will be competitive tomorrow after a good first day of running.' On that morrow Barrichello took pole from Schumacher who said 'the lap that counted for my grid position could have been better because I went off onto the grass'.

There was a chaotic start to the race, with much crashing at the first corner. 'I didn't see everything,' Schumacher would say, 'except that cars were flying everywhere.' The afternoon settled, Schumacher versus Montoya in the Williams and it finished like that, Schumacher murmuring about the perfect start to the season. So let's set out, progressively, Schumacher's domination as it unfolds.

Australia: Row 1 First Points: 10 Next: Montoya 6
Ferrari did not take the new Ferrari to Malaysia where on the Friday Schumacher was third and on the Saturday he took pole and said 'maybe I could have gone quicker if I

had waited to the very end of the session, but we chose to start my last run at the time we did because it seemed the best moment to avoid the traffic.' Montoya was alongside. Schumacher finished the race third although that was not without controversy because at the first corner he and Montoya bumped. 'Maybe Juan could have given me more room but he chose not to and we just touched. That's racing.' Neither he nor Montoya moved into the traditional rancour or recriminations – and Montoya's drive-through penalty was condemned as unfair on all sides. Schumacher pitted to change the front wing, resumed nineteenth and was *only* 1m 1s behind the winner, Ralf.

Malaysia Pole 3rd Points: 14 Next: Montoya 12
Schumacher was understood to be pushing hard for the new car for Brazil. Two days after Malaysia, Barrichello drove it for the first time, covering 78 laps round Barcelona. Two days after that Schumacher did 70 laps, next day a full race distance of 85 laps. Nobody doubted the F2002's speed, and now it had proved reliable. They'd take it to Sao Paulo for the Grand Prix.

On the Friday there Schumacher was fifth – 'we are learning all the time.' Next day he put it on the front row (Montoya pole) and won the race although that was not without controversy because Montoya claimed Schumacher chopped him. Montoya was attacking and Schumacher did move across to defend. Montoya had to pit and was very unhappy afterwards, particularly since Schumacher wasn't punished. Montoya made dark noises about the future, Brawn appealed for calm and Schumacher said 'I went for the inside line to leave him the outside.' He also said 'I believe we will get more reasonable with each other rather than hot-headed.'

Brazil   Row 1   First   Points: 24   Next: R Schumacher 16

Imola was as straightforward as it gets, Schumacher fastest on the wet Friday (from Barrichello): only Schumacher in the 1m 36s, only Barrichello in the 1m 37s. Pole (from Barrichello) on the Saturday and this: 'My team-mate really pushed me. When I start the race, I will have competed in more races for Ferrari than another other driver. That means a lot to me as it shows the mutual confidence we have.'

Enzo had lived by political intrigue, genius and, as it would seem, a complete lack of understanding of how other human beings work. Hence the high turnover of drivers and the mighty investment which for so long had produced so little. As we've seen in **Facts of the matter** at the end of Chapter Five, between 1992 – the arrival of di Montezemolo – and 2002, Ferrari had been transformed into a team with a modern, multi-national outlook based entirely on pragmatism. It had grown up.

Quite how *much* Schumacher felt on the eve of the San Marino Grand Prix is unclear. History still did not stir him in any active sense: gazing ahead, at Monza in 2003 he would drive the fastest Grand Prix of all and would say that it didn't interest him, only the 10 points for the win. At Imola, when the red lights went off to start the race, he certainly wasn't thinking about Ascari, Berger, Hawthorn, Scheckter, Surtees...

He led every lap of the race except two – refuelling – and beat Barrichello by 17.90 seconds. Now listen to the multi-national employee ticking off the topics: 'There are many reasons to be proud today. We failed here last year and now we have given something back to the *tifosi*. It was a special Grand Prix for me and I'm proud of the way it went. It was right that Rory Byrne should be on the podium. He is unique, very motivated and a great person. We did not expect to be so dominant. Bridgestone has produced a tyre that is more consistent and although the win was down to the whole package it was mainly due to the tyres. We will enjoy a glass of champagne to celebrate but at this early stage in the season we are already thinking about the next race in Spain and we start testing again on Tuesday.'

San Marino: Pole   First   Points: 34   Next: R Schumacher 20

Spain was even more straightforward in that he did not lose the lead at all even during his two pit stops. He was (naturally) quickest on the Friday; again on the Saturday – from Barrichello – and he 'enjoyed this session and the fight with Rubens. It was a challenge, especially as he was quicker on the first two runs. I looked at his sector and corner times to see where I could improve. Sometimes you think you are going flat out and your team-mate shows you that you are not.' He raced the spare car (his had a hydraulic problem) and said, without a trace of irony, 'although I was out in front I was not bored because I was able to watch the fight for sixth' – in the final few laps.

Spain: Pole   First   Points: 44   Next: Montoya 23

Austria convulsed Formula 1. To dispense with the preliminaries: he was second to Barrichello on the Friday; third – Barrichello on pole – next day; Barrichello drove a magnificent race, Schumacher following him home. As they approached the finishing line Barrichello suddenly slowed, as he had been ordered to do on the radio, gifting the win to Schumacher. The margin, 0.182 seconds, was meaningless. It was also drowned by the howls of protest mingled with catcalls which greeted Schumacher on the podium, and the vilification which surrounded the Ferrari team. That Schumacher refused to mount the top step of the podium, vacating it for Barrichello, seemed a gesture of contrition or sportsmanship or commiseration or something.

He would say: 'I take no joy from this victory. I enjoyed the race but not the last hundred metres. Only at the end was I called on the radio and told Rubens would move over.

The stunning amphitheatre of Austria, Barrichello seemingly on his way to victory – and Grand prix racing about to go volcanic.

Ferrari order Barrichello to pull over and let Schumacher win the Austrian GP.

A most unhappy place: the podium in Austria, Barrichello 'promoted' to the top rung.

A different mood althogether. The history parade in Canada.

I know the decision is not popular but imagine if we had lost the championship by this number of points at the end of the season. The team would look stupid in that situation.'

Because this book is about Schumacher's place in history, let's set what happened in an historical context. It might tell us a great deal.

At the 1955 British Grand Prix at Aintree, the works Mercedes of Moss and Fangio were dominant, to use the theme word of this chapter. Moss won by two-tenths of a second and is unsure to this day whether or not Fangio allowed him to: Moss the Briton winning his home race. Moss would not be surprised if Fangio had done so because, as he says, Fangio was like that. A gentleman.

At Monza in 1956, last race of the season, Englishman Peter Collins had a chance of the championship but Fangio, his team-mate at Ferrari, had a better one. Fangio's car broke down. Collins pitted and voluntarily handed his own car over to him (not illegal: you shared the points). Fangio said it was a gesture he would never forget, went out and took the championship.

Perhaps the championship then was a more gentlemanly thing altogether. Consider. In the early 1960s, another gentleman, Rob Walker, was able to finance his own Grand Prix team and run Moss in it. Compare that with *any* Formula 1 team today.

The first car to carry a sponsor's livery (Lotus/JPS) was not until 1968, when the big money began to roll. Grand Prix racing, which up to then had been concerned with life and death, now had a further dimension: raising money.

In 1982, some of the old values still obtained. Gilles Villeneuve felt betrayed by Ferrari team-mate Didier Pironi at Imola because the traditional Ferrari edict was that whichever of their drivers led, the other followed. Villeneuve had been leading and, when Pironi overtook, assumed it was to entertain the crowd – this was the time of the FISA/FOCA warfare and towards the end only four of the 14 starters were left. After some jousting Villeneuve further assumed that the fun was over. Then Pironi overtook him again, leaving Villeneuve no time to respond.

Villeneuve never spoke to him again.

That same year the Renault team held out boards ordering René Arnoux to slow and allow Prost to catch and overtake him in the French Grand Prix, because Prost had a better chance at the championship. Arnoux refused, and France went into a convulsion.

First point: the 1950s were now only memory and exercised no influence at all. Second point: Ferrari were a *racing* team and a company which made production cars that you could *race* on the roads. Third point: Renault were a vast semi-nationalised concern which was spending French taxpayers money to win the championship with a French driver (Arnoux and Prost were both French, of course) to proclaim *we are the best*. The French Grand Prix had been the eleventh of sixteen, Prost was on 19 points, Arnoux 4. The thing had tilted towards where we are now.

Fourth point: at the 1986 British Grand Prix at Brands Hatch, Mansell – contractually No. 2 driver to Nelson Piquet – led from Piquet and Frank Williams refused to give Mansell any signals. You cannot, he told me later, stand on a man's career. It went deeper than that. Like Enzo Ferrari, Williams was a racer. He'd apply team orders only when one of his drivers couldn't win the championship and, even then, reluctantly. At one race in 2003, when Montoya and Ralf both had a chance of the title, Williams was asked if he had given them orders? 'Yes,' he said. '*Race!*'

Ron Dennis at McLaren is very much the same. True, there'd been Senna's arrangement with Prost in 1989 at Imola – so they didn't crash in the first few corners – but Dennis didn't know about that. True in Australia in 1998 Coulthard had allowed Häkkinen through because they'd struck an agreement that whoever led at the first corner would win. This was so they didn't hound each other to destruction but protect the reliability of their new cars. As it happened, after a radio mis-communication about pitting, Coulthard led, kept his word and Häkkinen went by at the end. This agreement was due for the first two races of the season only.

Fifth point: although Williams and McLaren had intimate financial links with their engine manufacturers (BMW/Mercedes), they were not bound by any multi-national's corporate thinking. They guarded their own culture, which was the racing.

Sixth point: Ferrari had long been owned by a multi-national, Fiat, and, however tempted you are to see Italy as a glorious fairground of emotions, some very sharp-eyed and numerate people at Fiat watched – even though di Montezemolo would claim that the team was 'self-financed' (through sponsorship and road car sales).

This summer of 2002, Fiat were in financial difficulties and sold 34% of their Ferrari holding to an investment bank for £500 million, and that bank sold 10% on to another bank for £147m. We are talking big business and who can doubt that Schumacher's championships in the Ferrari were not a significant part of it?

The outrage in Austria was that Ferrari had not needed to make Barrichello gift his win to Schumacher who was so dominant that the season was tedious enough already, the integrity of the races had now been removed and Ferrari had thus brought the sport into disrepute. But most of all perhaps, the feeling was that Schumacher was so big he could have

Schumacher always insists it's a team effort. This is part of the team in action at Silverstone, where he won.

refused to overtake Barrichello. Brawn summed it up: 'We told the drivers [early on] we didn't want them racing. That's the nature of F1.' Frank Williams could never have spoken those words *at the sixth race of seventeen* and, even mindful of the Coulthard-Häkkinen debacle, I don't think Ron Dennis could either. What Brawn meant, whether he realised it or not, was that this was the true nature of the multi-national when applied to sport.

It is a nightmarish balance between the cost of money to win a championship and the cost of keeping the effort kissed by the purity of *sport*. If you don't have enough money you can't play, but if the thing really is about money then it only appears in the financial pages of the newspapers and dies, lost amid the fat cats, thin cats, foreign exchanges, stocks, shares, takeovers and stressed men in suits. There is no TV coverage of any of this happening (except specialist financial programmes spewing statistics) and for a reason. Nobody wants to watch it.

On 12 May 2002, Ferrari got the balance horribly wrong and Schumacher had to face it out at the press conference afterwards. Normally these are so mechanical that you'd swear it was a puppet show. Now, the press conference fully alive, Schumacher could be nothing but defensive. He refused to answer the final three questions,

which were: Isn't this a sport? Do you want to win because you are the best driver or have the best contract? If it's a team sport, why have individual champions?

The nightmare engulfed Schumacher and the two parts of the balance ground roughly against each other. On the podium, Schumacher visibly suffered in the name of sport while, nearby, the leading Ferrari personnel insisted they had done entirely the right thing *and would do it again.*

I think Schumacher conducted himself with admirable tact, restraint and dignity because presumably he didn't ask for team orders, he was informed of the corporate decision and, by implication, *he* was ordered to go by when Barrichello pulled over.

Should he have refused? Which employee thinks like that when a vast team effort is in play, the Fiat bean counters are fretting and the fear must surface: what if you do lose the championship by a point? He said 'Rubens did a superb job and he outpaced me all weekend.' Schumacher may be many things but he is not knowingly insincere.

Austria: Row 2 First Points: 54 Next: Montoya 27

At Monaco, Schumacher qualified third and finished second behind Coulthard. 'I kept pushing right to the end because in Monaco you never know what can happen, but David drove well and never gave me a chance.'

Monaco: Row 2 Second Points: 60
Next: R Schumacher, Montoya 27

Montoya took pole in Canada, Schumacher next to him. Schumacher was on a one-stop strategy – Barrichello and Montoya on two – and ran third behind them until the stops. Montoya re-took the lead when Schumacher finally pitted (lap 38) and led to his second stop. After that he hunted Schumacher and was beginning to catch him when, on lap 57, the engine let go. 'I kept a good pace because we knew Montoya was on a two-stop but I could not ease up until I knew I would be in front of him after his second stop.'

It was Ferrari's 150th win, and Schumacher – with Fangio's five championship record now almost in reach – uncharacteristically moved into an historical context. He described Fangio's feat as 'incomparable. I have a lot of respect for what he did, and I think that what we are doing now doesn't even come close to it.'

Canada: Row 1 First Points: 70
      Next: R Schumacher, Montoya 27

By something approaching irony, Barrichello had a very good European Grand Prix at the Nürburgring, leading every lap while Schumacher was behind him virtually the whole way. 'Why was Rubens not asked to let me by? The situation was very different to Austria. Now we are in a much stronger position.' Both Todt and Brawn confirmed that this was the team's thinking although, on the eve of Ferrari appearing before the FIA's World Council over Austria, Brawn added that they would continue to apply team orders if they felt it desirable.

Europe: Row 2 Second Points: 76 Next: R Schumacher 30

The World Council met in Paris, heard evidence and could not find a way of punishing Ferrari except for the podium offence of Barrichello being on the top step. They were fined £320,000 for this.

Schumacher qualified third at Silverstone, Montoya pole and leading the race until rain fell. The drivers pitted and,

of the two tyre companies, Bridgestone was the one to have – Brawn decided on intermediates. With them Schumacher was several seconds a lap quicker than Montoya and overtook him on lap 16. The race was over (although Barrichello, starting from the back of the grid after a problem on the warm-up lap, finished second). Schumacher could now take the championship in France.

Britain Row 2 First Points: 86 Next: Barrichello 32

Between Silverstone and Magny-Cours, Schumacher tested improvements to the Ferrari at Fiorano. On one day he did 107 laps with a best time of 57.47s, some 0.8 of a second faster than his own lap record. He said he wanted to 'get the title off our backs as soon as possible'. To do that he needed to win the race, with Montoya and Barrichello finishing no higher than third.

At Magny-Cours, he qualified on the front row (Montoya pole) and spoke in guarded terms about the race – 'I think it will be much closer than the last ones.'

Every race which can decide a championship has an

inherent element of drama. Small moments have big consequences. As the cars moved off on the formation lap Barrichello – second row – sat immobile, his Ferrari up on its jacks. The mechanics had been unable to fire the engine and Barrichello was out.

As the red lights went off Montoya made the better start, carving across to keep Schumacher behind him and they moved out into the country like that, Räikkonen third. Schumacher laid heavy pressure on Montoya and they duelled, Räikkönen trying to search out an opening as they did. Montoya stretched away and, as is the way in modern Grand Prix racing, the three ran equidistant towards the first pit stops.

Montoya pitted on lap 24 and the stop took 8.4 seconds stationary. Schumacher attacked the circuit for two laps – 1m 15.3, 1m 15.4. Montoya had done a 1m 15.9 on his lap exiting the pits. Schumacher pitted: 8.4 seconds stationary. As Schumacher emerged, Montoya was bearing down on him at ferocious speed. To get onto the track faster, Schumacher cut fractionally across the end of the white tramlines from the pits. He did hold Montoya, stretched away from him. Ten laps later Schumacher was given a 'drive-through' penalty for crossing the line. He emerged third behind Montoya and Räikkönen.

The championship would have to wait until the next race, Germany. Schumacher thought *it's all over for here.*

He attacked Räikkönen because, thinking tactically, he needed Räikkönen behind him so that the second pit stops would be like the first: Schumacher gaining enough time on a clear track to retake the lead when the stops were done. Räikkönen resisted.

Montoya pitted, 11.6 seconds stationary. Five laps later Schumacher pitted, 8.8 seconds stationary. Räikkönen pitted, 8.7 seconds stationary, and emerged just in front of Schumacher who swarmed all over him. Räikkönen, most phlegmatic of men, was unmoved. Montoya, meanwhile, struggled with the balance of the Williams and ran fourth, drifting back.

Schumacher 'took it a bit easy and then started to push

He equalled Fangio's record of five titles in France but en route to the race the track caught him out.

This is Indianapolis but it could have been anywhere: Fangio was famous, Schumacher became a global image – like this.

with ten laps to go'. On lap 68 of 72 he was close and at the Adelaide hairpin Räikkönen turned in very deep – he'd slithered on oil left by the Toyota of Allan McNish, which had just given up. Räikkönen got the McLaren back on track but by then Schumacher was through.

'Seeing him in trouble helped to warn me,' Schumacher would say. 'That's why I was able to change my line.' He had a moment or two of alarm when he realised he'd overtaken Räikkönen under a yellow flag and before he reached a green flag. He would not be punished for this.

The final laps were 'the worst of my life because I realised the championship was again in my pocket. I had a weight on my shoulders and felt enormous pressure not to make a mistake.'

He didn't.

'As I took the flag I felt an outburst of emotion and realised how much it means and how I love the sport.'

France: Row 1 First Points: 96 Next: Montoya 34

Facing a thicket of microphones in the paddock he confessed, his face betraying bemusement, that he felt so emotional he wasn't quite sure what to say.

L'Equipe compressed that perfectly with a headline across their front page above a photograph of Schumacher, arms raised, mouth seeming to bay in triumph:

ALONE WITH FANGIO

Schumacher would say 'I don't want to get into comparisons' when somebody mentioned Fangio, but Niki Lauda was quite prepared to, saying Schumacher was the greatest of all. More to the point, he was full of running and might set records which would last generations.

Schumacher won Germany, was second in Hungary, won Belgium, was second in Italy, was second in the USA and won Japan. No other driver had even been on the podium after every race of a season. His eleven victories were a record, beating the previous tally of nine (1995, 2000, 2001) he'd shared with Mansell (1992). His points total of 144 beat his own record, 123, set the season before. His winning margin – 67 – over the next man in the championship, Barrichello, beat his own record of 58 set the season before.

He had 64 wins, Prost next on 51. He had 945 points, Prost next on 798.5. He had 50 pole positions, only 15 behind Senna's record total. More than all that, he'd said when he won in France that 'it is not records that challenge me, it is the races. I do not feel I have achieved everything I want in my life and I will carry on treating each race as a new challenge.'

That is how he insisted he was approaching 2003, and it worked. You do not look at championships, you break them down in to their component parts, which are the races. In this way if you have a strong run, as he did in 2003 – pole and victory at successive races, Imola, Spain and Austria – you dismiss that from your thinking and concentrate *only* on the next race. In this same way, if you finish seventh in Germany and are lapped in Hungary – again successive races – you dismiss *that* from your thinking and concentrate on the next race, Monza. Pole there, victory there, and history beckoned.

And so, on a grey late afternoon in October, Barrichello cavorted on the Suzuka podium. Räikkönen and Coulthard were lost somewhere between solemnity and celebration – Räikkönen was second in the championship after all, but no racer likes to be second. Schumacher was nowhere to be seen. Eighth place did not entitle him to a place on the podium and so he didn't go up.

He didn't need to.

Instead, in his own time and in his own way, he could consider this: on 13 May 1950 at Silverstone, 21 cars set off to launch the World Championship. From there to Suzuka, 12 October 2003, there would be 713 Grands Prix, 91 different race winners [1] and 27 World Champions. We are talking about an astonishing panorama of skill, bravery, ambition and sometimes stark tragedy in some of the fastest racing cars man could make. It was something so basic that it exercised a global fascination and attracted some of the most interesting people on the planet to try and master it.

They were *all* behind Michael Schumacher now.

[1] This figure includes the winners of the Indianapolis 500, which until 1960 was counted as a round of the World Championship even though in drivers and machinery it was quite separate. I have left them in for reasons of completeness.

STATISTICS

Michael Schumacher's career as at 1 January 2004

Karting

1984 German Junior Champion

1985 German Junior Champion; Junior World Championship, 2nd

1986 German Senior Championship, 3rd; European Championship, 3rd

1987 German Senior Champion and European Champion

The cars

1988 Formula Koenig Champion; European Formula Ford, 2nd

1989 German F3, joint 2nd

1990 German F3 Champion; World Sports Car Championship, joint 5th; International F3, Macau, 1st; International F3, Fuji, 1st

1991 World Sports Car Championship, joint 9th; F1 début, Jordan, Benetton, 5 races. F1 drivers' championship, joint 12th

Grand Prix racing

1992 Benetton, 3rd (win, Belgium)

1993 Benetton, 4th (win, Portugal)

1994 Benetton, 1st (wins, Brazil, Pacific, San Marino, Monaco, Canada, France, Hungary, Belgium*, Europe)

1995 Benetton, 1st (wins, Brazil, Spain, Monaco, France, Germany, Belgium, Europe, Pacific, Japan)

1996 Ferrari, 3rd (wins, Spain, Belgium, Italy)

1997 Ferrari, 2nd ** (wins, Monaco, Canada, France, Belgium, Japan)

1998 Ferrari, 2nd (wins Argentina, Canada, France, Britain, Hungary, Italy)

1999 Ferrari, 5th (wins San Marino, Monaco)

2000 Ferrari, 1st (wins, Australia, Brazil, San Marino, Europe, Canada, Italy, USA, Japan, Malaysia)

2001 Ferrari, 1st (wins Australia, Malaysia, Spain, Monaco, Europe, France, Hungary, Belgium, Japan).

* Disqualified

** Excluded from the final classification for crashing into Jacques Villeneuve in Jerez).

The record-equalling year – 2002 Ferrari

3 Mar	Australia, Melbourne	1
17 Mar	Malaysia, Sepang	P/3
31 Mar	Brazil, Interlagos	1
14 Apr	San Marino, Imola	P/1
28 Apr	Spain, Barcelona	P/FL/1
12 May	Austria, A1-Ring	FL/1
26 May	Monaco, Monte Carlo	2
9 June	Canada, Montreal	1
23 June	Europe, Nürburgring	FL/2
7 July	Britain, Silverstone	1
21 July	France, Magny-Cours	1
28 July	Germany, Hockenheim	P/FL/1
18 Aug	Hungary, Hungaroring	FL/2
1 Sept	Belgium, Spa	P/FL/1
15 Sept	Italy, Monza	2
29 Sept	USA, Indianapolis	P/2
13 Oct	Japan, Suzuka	P/FL/1

Championship: Schumacher 144 points, Rubens Barrichello (Ferrari) 77, Juan Pablo Montoya (Williams) 50.

The record-breaking year – 2003 Ferrari

Date	Location	Result
9 Mar	Australia, Melbourne	P/4
23 Mar	Malaysia, Sepang	FL/6
6 Apr	Brazil, Interlagos	DNF
20 Apr	San Marino, Imola	P/FL/1
4 May	Spain, Barcelona	P/1
18 May	Austria, A1-Ring	P/FL/1
1 June	Monaco, Monte Carlo	3
15 June	Canada, Montreal	1
29 June	Europe, Nürburgring	5
6 July	France, Magny-Cours	3
20 July	Britain, Silverstone	4
3 Aug	Germany, Hockenheim	7
24 Aug	Hungary, Hungaroring	8
14 Sept	Italy, Monza	P/FL/1
28 Sept	USA, Indianapolis	FL/1
12 Oct	Japan, Suzuka	8

Championship: Schumacher 93, Kimi Räikkönen (McLaren) 91, Juan Pablo Montoya 82

Grand Prix totals

194 races: (David Hayhoe, *Grand Prix Data Book*, gives it as 195 – a fine point, because in 1996 in France the Ferrari expired on the formation lap)

Wins: 70 (world record, beating Alain Prost, 51)

Poles: 55

Fastest laps: 56 (world record, beating Prost, 41)

Points: 1038 (world record, beating Prost, 798.5)

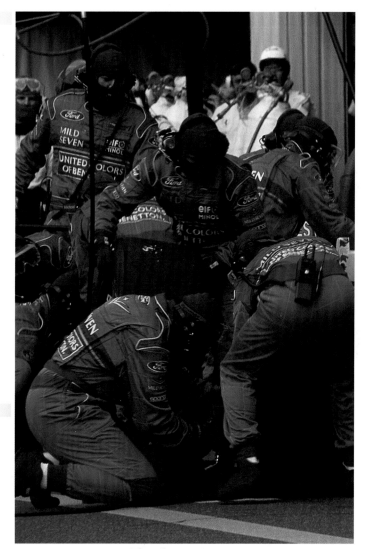

They don't say how many helpers you need to break records. Schumacher makes a pit stop in 1994 on the way to winning the Pacific Grand Prix at Aida, Japan.

INDEX